BUT THIS I KNOW

Also by George Austin

Affairs of State
Journey to Faith
Life of Our Lord

But this I know

Faith Hope and Love – A Meditation

George Austin, Archdeacon of York

Hodder & Stoughton

LONDON   SYDNEY   AUCKLAND

First published in Great Britain in 1996
by Hodder and Stoughton
A division of Hodder Headline PLC

10 9 8 7 6 5 4 3 2 1

British Library Cataloguing in Publication Data

A CIP catalogue record for this title is available
from the British Library

ISBN 0 340 64210 6

Typeset by Palimpsest Book Production Limited,
Polmont, Stirlingshire
Printed and bound in Great Britain by
Cox & Wyman, Reading, Berks

Hodder and Stoughton
A division of Hodder Headline PLC
338 Euston Road
London NW1 3BH

To our Lutheran friends
Bill and Sally White in Madison, Wisconsin,
and Sven-Oscar and Anna-Lisa Berglund
in Falkenberg, Sweden.

Contents

Acknowledgments

Biblical quotations throughout are from the Revised Standard Version, with the exception of those from the Book of Psalms, which are in Coverdale's translation from the *Book of Common Prayer*.

Preface

The idea for this book came during November 1994 while I was attending a preaching week at Wydale Hall, the York Diocesan Conference Centre, conducted by my good friend, Pastor William White, of Bethel Lutheran Church in Madison, Wisconsin. We were supposed to be producing a sermon, working alone, and I was pondering all Bill had said about the need to 'tell the story'. I thought of two chapters of my book, *Affairs of State*, in which I had written about the parable of the Prodigal Son and the story of the woman taken in adultery (both are reproduced in this book, in an expanded form, in chapters 12 and 13).

I had particularly enjoyed writing those chapters – why not try to do the same for the story of our salvation through Jesus Christ, in the Old and New Testaments? Then at evensong we sang the hymn, *I cannot tell*, which includes in each verse the phrase *But this I know*, contrasting the difficulty of belief with the understanding which comes of trust. I now had a pattern for the book – and its title.

Then something else which Bill said set in train the thoughts which produced the prose-poem fantasy with which I begin this exercise. Many of the chapters are expansions of ideas which I have already used in sermons. Our congregations need to hear the stories which enlighten faith; and we preachers need to tell them, for by so doing our own faith is enlightened.

I hope this little book will help members of study groups in

parishes and others who may use it in private to take their own
faith forward, and to realise that the message of Jesus Christ
truly is good news for all.

George Austin
St Valentine's Day, 1996

1

Oops! – a Fantasy

[I-the-Creator paused.]

The empty void,
  formless in chaos,
  became Light.
    Light dancing,
      advancing,
      pulsating,
      creating.

Creating form out of nothingness,
  reality out of vacuity,
  time amidst eternity.
    Light clustered in stars,
      stars in galaxies,
        twisting and curling,
      planets forming,
        cooling.

On one tiny dust speck,
  volcanoes disgorged new land and the earth quaked,
    composing mountains and valleys,
        seas and dry land,
        always changing.
  Creatures were shaped,
    designed and redesigned,
        to live in the seas and on the land.

[But I-the-Creator was not satisfied.]

'I create because I am Love
  and Love must create.
  All that I create reveals my Love.
    But nothing I have created can love as I do.
      As I AM.'

[I-the-Almighty saw that this was so.]

'Then unless I give the power to love
  to a creature I have made,
    my creation will be incomplete.'

[I-the-Wise saw that this was so.]

'But such a creature will be made in my image.
  For truly to have the power to love,
    the creature must also have the choice to love me
      or to reject me.'

[I-the-Almighty saw that this was so.]

'Such a choice is a great gift
  and a great power.
    For to have such a power
      the creature must also know how to choose
        between good
          and evil.'

[I-the-Creator saw that this was so.]

'It is a risk above all risks.

I am Love and that which I create is all Good.
But the creature will have power to invite Evil into my
creation.'

[I-the-Wise saw that this was so.]

'I have created the creature-who-can-Love.
Who at once prefers Evil to Good.
I would have filled him
with all my Fullness.

But the creature-who-can-Love chooses to turn away
from the Ground of his being,
from the Fulfiller of his purpose,
from the Love of his love.'

[I-the-Almighty saw that this was so.]

'I can take Love from him
and make him as all the other creatures.
But this I will not do
for I knew the risk
and I prepared the response.'

[I-the-Creator saw that this was so.]

'I am the Word which creates
and I only am the Word which can restore.
I will be born into my Creation as Word-made-Flesh
to redeem the creature-who-can-Love.'

[I-the-Wise saw that this was so.]

'I will be the Creature-who-is-Love.
        All will be redeemed.
        All will be sanctified.'

'I just can't believe it, doctor. I'd have trusted her completely
– a good, decent, honourable girl. And now this. Who's the
father? You might well ask. She won't say – or rather she's
made up some cock and bull story that it just happened, that
she's never been with a boy! Can you believe it? Girls these
days! An abortion, doctor? Well, I don't know, I don't like the
idea of taking a baby's life. It is my grandchild, after all. Oh, I
ought not to look at it like that? Think of it as a foetus? Well,
that doesn't sound quite so human. Yes, all right, I'll see she
comes to the clinic.'

[I-the-Creator paused.]

'They have killed the One who was the Word-made-Flesh.
        I know that I must enter suffering and death
            for their sakes.
      But Evil has taught them
            not only to kill but to stop life before birth
                and call it good so to do.'

[I-the-Almighty saw that this was so.]

'I can take Love from him
    and make him as all the other creatures.
        But this I will not do
            for I knew the risk
                and I prepared the response.'

[I-the-Creator saw that this was so.]

'From eternity I touched time
  when Evil had gained great power over the creature-who-
  can-Love.

  I will touch an earlier time for my purpose.'

Now the birth of Jesus Christ took place in this way. When his
mother Mary had been betrothed to Joseph, before they came
together she was found to be with child of the Holy Spirit; and
her husband Joseph, being a just man and unwilling to put her
to shame, resolved to divorce her quietly. But as he considered
this, behold, an angel of the Lord appeared to him in a dream,
saying, 'Joseph, son of David, do not fear to take Mary your
wife, for that which is conceived in her is of the Holy Spirit;
and she will bear a son, and you shall call his name Jesus, for
he will save his people from their sins.'

2

But this I know

Faith is knowing yet not always understanding: a conjunction of belief and trust. It is a confidence in the knowledge that God is to be trusted, in His promises, in His love and in the truths He has revealed, while at the same time recognising that the human mind is too small to comprehend in all His fullness the One who is creator of all things.

I see the stars in the vastness of the heavens and know that their light, travelling at light's speed, has yet taken millions of years to reach me. And there are myriads of other stars at the edge of our universe beyond the vision of the largest telescope. Perhaps myriads of other universes too, all created by the one God. It would be the most monstrous arrogance to expect to understand such a God in His omnipotence and in His majesty.

It is just such an arrogance that the Lord challenges in Job:

'Where were you,' He asks of Job, 'when I laid the
    foundation of the earth?
    Tell me, if you have understanding.
Who determined its measurements – surely you know!
    Or who stretched the line upon it?
On what were its bases sunk,
    or who laid its cornerstone,
when the morning stars sang together,
    and all the sons of God shouted for joy?' (Job 38:4–7)

Could I possibly understand how God knows this speck of dust on which we live, in a far corner of this universe, or how He could care for me so much that He would choose to enter His creation as the child of a young virgin? Yet I have felt His love, known His guidance, tasted His presence, been comforted by Him in many troubles, had my way enlightened by Him in the valley of the shadow of death. He has never failed me and I know His word is to be trusted.

So I believe that He was born of a virgin bride, though I cannot reason how this could be, how Mary could conceive before she came together with Joseph. Some would say that Scripture provides little evidence, though in an age of story-telling, the birth narratives could have been kept in the heart of Mary to be told and re-told. His enemies were later to challenge him with the words, 'We were not born of fornication' (John 8:41), perhaps a hint of a continuing and commonly known question about his origins.

The virginal conception of Jesus remains a mystery of God, unprovable, to be accepted only in faith. Far more important is the truth that this child is the Word of God made flesh, come to 'save his people from their sins' (Matthew 1:21). In the sublime words which open the gospel according to St John:

In the beginning was the Word, and the Word was with God, and the Word was God. He was in the beginning with God; all things were made through him, and without him was not anything made that was made. In him was life, and the life was the light of men.

And the Word became flesh and dwelt among us, full of grace and truth: we have beheld his glory, glory as of the only Son from the Father. (John 1:1–4,14)

But this I know, that He was born of Mary,
when Bethlehem's manger was His only home,
and that He lived at Nazareth and laboured,
and so the Saviour, Saviour of the world, is come.

I know too that this holy child will die by crucifixion, just outside the gates of the city of Jerusalem, a remote and inhospitable city on the edge of the vastness of the Roman Empire. He was by no means the only victim of this horrible form of death, a prolonged and agonising punishment for a noted evil-doer. Indeed his suffering was shared by two thieves, receiving, as one admitted, 'the just reward' of their misdeeds. Nor was he the first or the only prophet of Israel to have been rejected by his own people, and not the first to be killed by them. But no event in history was more important, for by this death our broken relationship with the God who made us and loves us could be restored and repaired. For we are to believe that this prophet of God is more than that, that He is God incarnate, the Word become flesh for our sakes.

> *The Word in the bliss of the Godhead remains,*
> *Yet in flesh comes to suffer the keenest of pains;*
> *He is that he was, and for ever shall be,*
> *But becomes that he was not, for you and for me.*

Another mystery of God which human reason cannot explain and hardly explore.

> *But this I know, He heals the broken-hearted,*
> *and stays our sin, and calms our lurking fear,*
> *and lifts the burden from the heavy-laden,*
> *for yet the Saviour, Saviour of the world, is here.*

I know too that this holy child is the Christ–Messiah, the Prince of Peace, here to establish his kingdom of justice and righteousness. I know that he heralds the age presaged by Isaiah when

> the wolf shall dwell with the lamb,
>   and the leopard shall lie down with the kid,
> and the calf and the lion and the fatling together,
>   and a little child shall lead them.

The cow and the bear shall feed;
  their young shall lie down together;
  and the lion shall eat straw like the ox.
The sucking child shall play over the hole of the asp,
  and the weaned child shall put his hand on the adder's
  den.
They shall not hurt nor destroy in all my holy mountain;
for the earth shall be full of the knowledge of the Lord,
  as the waters cover the sea. (Isaiah 11:6–9)

The promise is not of joy in the next world to compensate for misery in this, 'an opium-dose' – in Charles Kingsley's words – 'for keeping beasts of burden patient while they are being overloaded.' Yet I know that after two thousand years we live in a world of violence. After dark, parts of our cities are no-go areas for the weak and vulnerable, children are abused and mistreated, women are raped and people are robbed, sometimes in full view of a public too fearful to intervene.

Internationally, genocide is not part of history but a fact of today: man's gross inhumanity to man did not end with the defeat of Nazism in 1945. And without the extremes of ethnic cleansing, wars continue to rage, smaller perhaps but no less bloody, with the death of a son or a father no less devastating and tragic because the conflict in which it occurred was no more than a minor story in the corner of the world news.

But despite the wars which still darken our world, there is another, a more hopeful, picture. Who could have foreseen only ten years ago that the Cold War would be over, that East and West would no longer threaten mutual annihilation; or that the evil of communism which had enslaved the people of Eastern Europe and the Soviet Union would so quickly collapse; or that in South Africa the wickedness of apartheid would have been overcome without a bloodbath?

And fifty years ago it would have seemed a foolish optimism to suggest that whatever the political difficulties still to be overcome, the great nations of Europe would now be living in one community with the slaughter of the two Great Wars a history never to be repeated. It is by no means a hope against hope now to suggest that the eventuality of war between Britain, France and Germany is now as remote as a repetition of the wars in England between Yorkists and Lancastrians.

We learn, even if we learn slowly: and the day of the Prince of Peace comes nearer. Yet in the limits of our human comprehension, we can be forgiven if we see only the conflicts. The very society in which we live seems sometimes to be on the verge of disintegration, as the forces of law and order appear unable to cope and morality is disregarded or undermined. It is all so far from the promise offered in the birth of the Holy Child of Bethlehem, so remote from the message of love which is at the heart of Christmas.

Yet my faith tells me that, whatever I see around me to bring despair, the battle has been won on the cross which was to end the earthly life of Jesus. I do not understand, cannot ever fully comprehend, how in Jesus God became man, the Word of God made flesh; nor how in dying for me he could restore the broken relationship between God and his people, the men, women and children whom He created in His image, with the ability to love, and to choose between good and evil. I cannot tell how in His own good time the nations will be won, or how He will claim his heritage and show us he is King.

> *But this I know, all flesh shall see His glory,*
> *and He shall reap the harvest He has sown,*
> *and some glad day His sun shall rise in splendour*
> *when He the Saviour, Saviour of the world is known.*

It is God's promise that all will be made new, that justice will triumph over inequity, righteousness over iniquity, all that is good over all that is evil, but I cannot tell how this can be, even though I know that on the cross of Christ the final battle was fought and won. And yet I know His promise is true, and that the revelation to St John the Divine will be fulfilled.

Then I saw a new heaven and a new earth;

for the first heaven and the first earth were passed away,
and the sea was no more.
And I saw the holy city, new Jerusalem,
coming down out of heaven from God,
prepared as a bride adorned for her husband;
and I heard a great voice from the throne saying,
'Behold the dwelling of God is with men.
He will dwell with them,
and they shall be his people,
and God will be with them;
he will wipe away all tears from their eyes,
and death shall be no more,
neither shall there be mourning nor crying nor pain
any more,
for the former things are passed away.'
And he who sat upon the throne said,
'Behold, I make all things new.' (Revelation 21:1–5)

It is beyond my human limitations to encompass the truth that there will indeed be 'a new heaven and a new earth', when 'death shall be no more, neither shall there be mourning nor crying nor pain any more'. I cannot comprehend how God can make all things new, that in that day, all will know the God revealed in Jesus and rejoice in that knowledge.

But this I know, the skies will fill with rapture,
and myriad, myriad human voices sing,
and earth to heaven, and heaven to earth, will answer:
At last the Saviour, Saviour of the world, is King!

3

Glory and Creation

The end of the story is the promise of a 'new heaven and a new earth'. We must return to the beginning; and the beginning is Genesis, with the two stories of creation. Look for historical or scientific truth in these two sublime accounts and the theological truths which the writers sought to convey in poetic form will be obscured. Dismiss the stories as no more than the mythology of ancient peoples, and fundamental truths of God will be lost or undermined.

But to reject the picture of God there displayed will be a denial which will eat away at the power of scripture to determine a right approach to doctrine, morality, ministry, worship – indeed to all that makes the faith of a Christian live and relevant. And that faith begins with an awareness that all around us we see the power and love of a God who created all things.

> In the beginning God created the heavens and the earth. The earth was without form and void, and darkness was upon the face of the deep; and the Spirit of God was moving over the face of the waters. And God said, 'Let there be light'; and there was light. (Genesis 1:1–3)

It is no accident that the evangelist John begins his gospel account with an echo of those opening words of the Old

Testament, for his too is a story of creation, of the divine Word who is God and is with God from the beginning as the instrument and means of all creativity. As in Genesis, where the light comes into being at God's word, so in John the life of God brings light to all mankind.

In the beginning was the Word, and the Word was with God, and the Word was God. He was in the beginning with God; all things were made through him, and without him was not anything made that was made. In him was life, and the life was the light of men. The light shines in darkness, and the darkness has not overcome it. (John 1:1–5)

As it was by the word of God – 'And God *said*' – that creation was enacted, so Jesus, the light of the world, the way, the truth and the life, is that Word of God, Word made flesh: 'And the Word became flesh and dwelt among us, full of grace and truth; we have beheld his glory, glory as of the only son from the Father' (John 1:14).

The same theme is to be found in the opening of John's first Epistle, where he speaks of that which forms the proclamation of the Good News, the gospel of Jesus Christ: 'That which was from the beginning, which we have heard, which we have seen with our eyes, which we have looked upon and touched with our hands, concerning the word of life . . .' (1 John 1:1).

St Paul too, in the first chapter of his Letter to the Ephesians – an epistle which could be described as the gospel according to Paul – opens with a hymn of praise to God, creator, redeemer and sanctifier. It is the Father

who has blessed us in Christ
    with every spiritual blessing in the heavenly places,
    even as he chose us in him before the foundation of
      the world,
    that we should be holy and blameless before him.

He destined us in love to be his sons through Jesus Christ,
     according to the purpose of his will,
          to the praise of his glorious grace.

(Ephesians 1:3–6)

So Paul proclaims the eternal relationship which the Creator
intended to share with the creature whom He made in His
divine image as a creature-who-can-Love. That we are not
'holy and blameless' is not the end of the dream, for his Love
is too great for that.

In him we have redemption through his blood,
     the forgiveness of our trespasses,
          according to the riches of his grace which he lavished
          upon us.
In him, according to the purpose of him who accomplishes
     all things
          according to the purpose of his will,
we who first hoped in Christ
     have been destined and appointed to live
          for the praise of his glory. (Ephesians 1:7–12)

The Spirit, who in Genesis 'moved upon the face of the
waters', is the active Love of God among His people, giving
assurance of all His promises and to His people, the grace to
fulfil His purposes.

In him you also,
     who heard the word of truth,
     the gospel of your salvation,
          were sealed with the promised Holy Spirit,
which is the guarantee of our inheritance until we acquire
     possession of it,
          to the praise of his glory. (Ephesians 1:11–12)

In 1960, I was assistant chaplain in the University of London, under that eccentric priest and formidable preacher, Prebendary Gordon Phillips, and I well remember his advice to a colleague who was appointed to preach the university sermon on the Sunday after Pentecost. 'Don't preach on the Trinity. No-one should ever try to preach on the doctrine of the Trinity.'

Yet the Trinity of three Persons in one God is at the heart of the revelation of God which Christian tradition has developed. It must have a meaning which enlightens our understanding of God, or it would not be there. I believe that meaning lies in the words of St John in his first Letter. 'God is love, and he who abides in love abides in God, and God abides in him' (1 John 4:16).

If God is Love then He must display the three-fold characteristic which is always present in love: the lover, the beloved and the act of love which proceeds from the one to the other. Love is always a transitive verb: we cannot say, 'I love' without provoking the question, 'But what do you love?' Love must have an object: another person, music, sport, art or whatever. And it must encompass activity.

'You say you love music. Do you play an instrument? No? – then do you listen to music on the radio or have a collection of CDs? No? – then surely you must go to concerts. No?' So the claim, 'I love music' without activity becomes a nonsense. So God, lover and beloved, without that activity of love which is the Holy Spirit, proceeding forth from Father and Son, is an impossibility.

God is undoubtedly the Lover, for all that he performs in creation and redemption displays that love. He is too the Beloved, of whom the voice from heaven at the baptism of Jesus declared: 'This is my Son, the Beloved in whom I am well pleased' (Matthew 3:17). And he is the act and activity of Love which proceeds between Father and Son, and proceeds from both into creation as the source of all love.

It is because God is Love that he is concerned for and involved in his creation. So from an inspired but early revelation of God the Creator in the opening verses of the Bible – a God who created order out of chaos by the power of his word, whose spirit moved over the face of the waters – we have come to a no less inspired and early revelation of God as the most holy and undivided Trinity of Father, Son and Holy Spirit, whose actions are always 'to the praise of his glory'.

'Glory' is an important and highly significant theological word, and in his magisterial work, *The Glory of God and Transfiguration of Christ* (Longmans, 1949), Michael Ramsey shows its crucial importance in understanding the nature and purpose of God as revealed in holy Scripture. He points out that in the Old Testament 'glory' signifies two aspects of God. It shows his character as revealed by his acts in history, as in the book Numbers where the Lord speaks of 'the men who have seen my glory and my signs which I wrought in the wilderness' (Numbers 14:22); and it is also seen in physical phenomena which make God's presence known.

This is reflected particularly in the imagery of thunder, lightning, earthquake, fire, volcanic action which is so often employed by writers in the Old and to a lesser extent in the New Testament. It is hardly surprising that this should be so, for unleashed natural power is a fearsome sight. On 18 May 1980, at 8.27 a.m., Mount St Helens in Washington State exploded in a vast eruption which by 8.33 had blasted away the equivalent of the mass of Ben Nevis from the mountain's top. To see it now against a pattern of its former height one can only marvel at the awesome power in nature. It is little wonder that for Old Testament writers such phenomena became metaphors for the power and glory of God.

Yet alongside such frightening images, God's glory is also in his caring presence among the beings he has created. Here is no divinity who, having created all things and made man in his own image, then abandons his creation like a discarded toy and leaves unsupported mankind to a slippery slope of self-destruction. Rather he is a God who cares, who is involved, who intervenes, and who is present with his creation.

'My presence will go with you, and I will give you rest.'

And Moses said, 'If thy presence will not go with me, do not carry us up from here. For how shall it be known that I have found favour in thy sight, I and thy people? Is it not in going with us, so that we are distinct, I and thy people, from all the other people that are upon the face of the earth?' (Exodus 33:14–16).

Here is a foretaste of the love of a God who will be the Word made Flesh, to dwell among us, whose glory we have seen, and whose promise is that he is with us 'always, to the close of the age' (Matthew 28:20).

Yet this is only one aspect of God's glory. For He whose presence goes with us, who can be discerned in the creation which is the work of his hands, is also beyond all things and all knowledge. He is the one of whom the seraphim in Isaiah's vision (Isaiah 6:3) sang: 'Holy, holy, holy is the Lord of hosts: the whole earth is full of his glory.'

There is here a remoteness from the unrighteousness of the world which affects the individual's perception of his relationship with God, as in Isaiah's response to the vision of glory: 'And I said, "Woe is me! For I am lost; for I am a man of unclean lips, and I dwell in the midst of a people of unclean lips; for my eyes have seen the King, the Lord of hosts!"' (Isaiah 6:5).

It influences too our understanding of God's sovereignty over His creation:

Every valley shall be exalted, and every mountain and hill made low;
and the crooked shall be made straight and the rough places plain;
And the glory of the Lord shall be revealed,
and all flesh shall see it together,
for the mouth of the Lord hath spoken it.'

(Isaiah 40:4–5)

And if that were not enough, it proclaims God's sovereignty over all the nations of the earth:

Arise, shine; for your light has come,
  and the glory of the Lord has risen upon you.
For behold, darkness shall cover the earth,
  and thick darkness the peoples;
but the Lord will arise upon you,
  and his glory will be seen among you.
And nations shall come to your light,
  and kings to the brightness of your rising.'

(Isaiah 60:1–3)

God is both over all and in all, and these two aspects of His glory must be held together in tension, in our understanding of God and in our worship of Him. As Ramsey says (*The Glory of God and Tranfiguration of Christ*, p. 22), the Bible speaks

on the one hand of Israel's transcendent king and judge and on the other hand of a presence tabernacling in Israel's midst . . . Always in tension, the contrasted aspects of the divine glory find their true unity when the Word by whom all things were made became flesh and dwelt among us, and the glory of Bethlehem and Calvary is the glory of the eternal God.

4

Creation and Sin

The first creation story in Genesis came out of the pain of exile when the children of Israel had been taken into slavery in Babylon and was a response to the real threat of absorption into the debased religions of their captors. The second (Genesis 2:4–3:24) comes from an earlier and more pastoral era, where the perfection of God's creation is to be found in the tranquillity of the Garden of Eden. Here man can find all that is necessary for sustenance and the only forbidden act is to eat of 'the tree of knowledge of good and evil' which is in the midst of the Garden.

It is a gentle, rustic story, beginning with a planet empty of life in any form. Then a mist rose, from which rain came to water the whole earth. God formed man out of the dust of the earth and breathed life into him. He was to live in the Garden of Eden, to till it and to keep it, able to eat an apparently vegetarian diet from the fruit of the trees which were in the Garden. But if he were to eat of the fruit of the tree of knowledge of good and evil he would surely die.

The beasts and birds were made by God and the Man named them all; but none was fit to be his companion. So God created Woman, a creature like Man himself, to be his companion. And there was in the Garden with them a serpent, a cunning creature, who asked the Woman, innocently, 'Did God really say to you that you cannot eat the fruit of any tree in the Garden?'

'No, no, you've got it wrong,' she replied. 'We *may* eat the fruit of the trees of the Garden. What we may *not* eat is the fruit of the tree which is in the midst of the Garden. God has told us that if we eat of that tree's fruit we shall die.'

The serpent laughed: 'That's rubbish! You won't die. But what will happen – as God knows – is that if you do eat of its fruit, you will be like God himself. You will know good and evil. Wouldn't that be wonderful?'

Indeed it would, the Woman argued to herself. Why, if we really knew good and evil, we could serve God all the better. And anyway, it is rather an attractive-looking fruit. So she gathered its fruit and ate; and she gave some to her husband, and he ate. Their eyes were opened and beauty was despoiled. What had been only good could now become evil. Desire became greed, and generosity was replaced by covetousness. Even love itself, even their love for each other, could become lust. The Man and the Woman knew that they were naked; and now, only now, did it embarrass them.

It was evening time, the cool of the day, and the Lord God walked in the Garden. But they hid from him, ashamed to meet the One who in love had given them all that was good.

'Where are you?' God asked.

The Man replied, 'I could hear you in the Garden and I was afraid, because I was naked. So I hid myself.'

Silence for a moment as God weighed the answer. Then He said, in a voice which thundered and echoed and re-echoed around the Garden: 'Naked? Naked? Who told you you were naked? Have you disobeyed my word and eaten of the fruit of the tree I ordered you, commanded you, not to eat?'

The Man replied: 'Well, yes. But it wasn't my fault: it was that Woman. She gave me of the fruit of the tree and I ate. And don't forget it was you who gave me the Woman in the first place.' The Woman simply blamed the serpent.

Sin is to disobey God's commandments; and the sin is compounded when we refuse to accept responsibility for our actions. The Man blamed the Woman, the first husband to blame his wife but by no means the last, and then blamed

God for putting him in the position of having a wife. It is an ancient story but a modern predisposition.

A man who inflicted terrible injuries on a baby is sent on an anger-management course, for babies can be tiresome, noisy little creatures; a woman kills a lover and is freed because she was suffering from pre-menstrual tension at the time; a violent rioter is given a lenient sentence because the police had shouted racist taunts. It is a characteristic of the society in which we live and it is the symptom of a sick society, a society in which sin is condoned and evil takes hold.

The refusal to take responsibility for our actions is to commit the sin of Adam, the sin by which he compounded the first sin, which was to disobey God's command. As punishment, the Man and the Woman were driven out of the Garden of Eden: but not only for punishment. For the Lord God said:

'Behold, the man has become like one of us, knowing good and evil; and now, lest he put forth his hand and take also of the tree of life, and eat, and live for ever' – therefore the Lord God sent him forth from the Garden of Eden, to till the ground from which he was taken. (Genesis 3:22–3)

And there is the dilemma. Eternal life is God's purpose for the creature made in His image, but by choosing evil rather than good, the creature is cut off, by his own act and choice, from God's intention. But the ability to choose is God's own gift to Man, the gift of free will, and if the relationship broken by sin is to be restored it must be through Man himself, if the gift of free will is not to be negated.

The Old and New Testaments, after the creation stories in Genesis, are the account of how God brings this about, a purpose which reaches its consummation in the birth, death and resurrection of the one who is the Word-made-Flesh, Jesus of Nazareth.

But this is pre-eminently the action of a God who is outside His creation rather than part of it. That all has been created by the one God gives creation a unity. In their profound revelation of God in creation, the Jewish writers would have none of the warring gods, conquerors and conquered, male and female, of the Babylonians among whom they lived and whose religion they would reject.

Not for them an ordered universe brought about by Marduk's victory over Tiamat, the female god of chaos and darkness, whose body is divided to form the firmament. The Jewish God creates all things, the heavens, the earth, light and darkness, the sun, moon and stars, animal life, vegetation, and finally, in God's own image, man himself.

> Then God said, 'Let us make man in our image, after our likeness; and let them have dominion over the fish of the sea, and over the birds of the air, and over the cattle, and over all the earth, and over every creeping thing that creeps upon the earth.' So God created man in his own image, in the image of God he created him; male and female he created them.' And God blessed them and said, 'Be fruitful and multiply.' (Genesis 1:26–8)

We call God 'he' because we cannot call Him 'it'; and we do not, if we are to remain Christian, call God both 'he' and 'she'. It is we who are made in God's image, not He in ours: He is not like us but we are like Him, creatures who can love as He loves and as He is. He is not a god with a human face, an old man in the clouds; nor is He male and female, for to describe Him as such is either to return to the paganism so studiously avoided by the Jewish theologians, or, once again, to make Him in our image and likeness. To fall into either trap is gross heresy, overturning and rejecting the biblical revelation where throughout, to avoid the heresies, God is addressed with the male pronoun, and where Jesus reveals Him as one who may be addressed as Abba, Father.

He is, in the words of the first of the Thirty-Nine Articles of Religion of the Anglican tradition, the 'one living and true God, everlasting, without body, parts, or passions; of infinite power, wisdom, and goodness; the Maker, and Preserver of all things both visible and invisible'.

The unity of creation is a unity in diversity, for the wonder of God in creation is in its diversity. St Paul has much to say about this in his Letter to the Ephesians, where God is the one who 'fills all in all': 'He has put all things under his [i.e. Christ's] feet, and has made him the head over all things for the church, which is his body, the fullness of him who fills all in all' (Ephesians 1:22–3).

Later Paul describes the unity which exists in the power of the spirit of God: 'There is one body and one Spirit, just as you were called to the one hope that belongs to your call, one Lord, one faith, one baptism, one God and Father of us all, who is above all and through all and in all' (Ephesians 4:4–6).

Yet God's gifts, like his gifts in creation, were marked by their diversity: 'And his gifts were that some should be apostles, some prophets, some evangelists, some pastors and teachers' (Ephesians 4:10–11).

It is with the divers riches of God's glory that we are to be strengthened with might, inwardly through his Spirit, in the words of St Paul's great prayer, which ends with the awesome promise that we are able to be 'filled with all the fullness of God':

That Christ may dwell in your hearts through faith; that you, being rooted and grounded in love, may have power to comprehend with all the saints what is the breadth and length and height and depth, and to know the love of Christ which surpasses knowledge, that *you may be filled with all the fullness of God*. (Ephesians 3:17–19)

This is indeed the fulfilment of God's purpose in creation, which cannot be thwarted because of the sin and disobedience which man's misuse of free will introduced into the goodness of that creation. And it is the ultimate proof of the love of God for his creation that He should choose to redeem us not because of what we are but in spite of what we have become.

5

The Presence of God

Whenever I read of God's promise in Ephesians, 'that you may be filled with all the fullness of God', it is such an awesome thought that it never fails to send a tingle down my spine. How may I, a sinner – even a sinner redeemed – be filled with all the fullness of Him who is creator of all things? What can it mean and how can it come to be? Even the perception that God goes with us throughout our journey in this life is mystery enough. Yet it is His promise, constantly made.

There have been times in my own life when God has seemed far away, dark periods in church affairs perhaps when doing the will of God in the particular task He has given me has seemed like trudging through a sea of near-impenetrable and quite unresponsive mud. More than once it has been my own 'valley of the shadow of death', in which the Shepherd–Lord has seemed far away if not entirely absent. In time, at the valley's end, I have learnt that He was with me throughout and that I could not have completed the journey without Him.

In the process, Psalm 23 has become not just a sentimental hymn to be sung at weddings and funerals but a pure description of a wonder of God, a developing knowledge that the Lord indeed is my shepherd:

He shall feed me in a green pasture:
    and lead me forth beside the waters of comfort.
He shall convert my soul:

and bring me forth in the paths of righteousness, for his
name's sake.
Yea, though I walk through the valley of the shadow of
death, I will fear no evil:
    for thou art with me; thy rod and thy staff comfort
    me.

                            (Psalm 23:2–4)

It is a promise echoed in that wonderful psalm of the
inescapable presence of God, Psalm 139:

Whither shall I go then from thy Spirit:
    or whither shall I go then from thy presence?
If I climb up into heaven, thou art there:
    if I go down to hell, thou art there also.
If I take the wings of the morning
    and remain in the uttermost parts of the sea;
Even there also shall thy hand lead me,
    and thy right hand shall hold me.
If I say, Peradventure the darkness shall cover me:
    then shall my night be turned to day.
Yea, the darkness is no darkness with thee, but the night is
as clear as the day:
    the darkness and light to thee are both alike.

                          (Psalm 139:6–11)

God's promise to Moses is a covenant with all his people:
'My presence shall go with thee, and I will give thee rest'
(Exodus 33:14). But human doubt is often stronger than faith,
so that the presence is not always discerned. Moses himself
was not to be excluded from that doubt, even though the Lord
would speak to him 'face to face, as a man speaks to his friend'
(Exodus 33:11).

For Moses responded as to a friend: 'Look, Lord, you keep
telling me that I must bring up your people to the Promised
Land. But I can't do it all on my own, and you won't tell me
who is going to be with me to help me. Yet you've said that

I've "found favour in your sight", whatever that might mean. Don't lead me up the garden path – show me how it's all going to happen. After all, this nation is supposed to be your chosen people.'

The Lord replied, in a word, 'My presence will go with you, and I will give you rest.'

'Don't say that if you don't mean it,' Moses replied. 'And don't let us go on from here unless your presence is with us. How will anyone know that we are your people, chosen from every other nation upon the earth, unless you go along with us?'

The Lord replied, 'This very thing you have spoken, I will do.'

Moses was still unsure, still demanding proof. 'I beg you, Lord, show me the glory which is your Presence.'

For a moment the Lord was silent. Then He said, 'I will make all my goodness pass before you, and will even proclaim before you my name, "The Lord". And I will be gracious to whom I will be gracious, and will show mercy on whom I will show mercy. But you cannot see my face; for no-one can see me and live.'

The Lord continued: 'See, there is a place by me where you shall stand upon the rock. While the glory which is my Presence passes by, I will put you in a cleft in the rock, and cover you with my hand until I have passed by. Then I will take away my hand and you shall see my back. But my face you will not see.' (From Exodus 33:12–23.)

Like Moses, we cannot see the glory of God in all its fullness. But sometimes a corner of the veil which separates us – nay, protects us – from that glory is lifted. It may be in the beauty of the natural world, where something seen for the first time or in a new light opens up a vision of God's glory in creation.

My wife and I took a small plane to see the Grand Canyon in northern Arizona. We flew at first over a snow-covered plateau dotted with Ponderosa pines until suddenly we were at the lip of the Canyon, a great, meandering gash two hundred miles long, sometimes fourteen miles across and a mile deep.

We were stunned by its grandeur: the carved rocky outcrops, the multi-coloured, layered deposits, clouds clinging to deep valleys below us, patches of snow against red, yellow, ochre rock, the sheer immensity of it all.

It was not the presence of God, it was not gouged out by a divine hand but by natural forces; but it was a reminder of the glory of God which empowers those forces. And it is the same glorious presence of God which endows us with the faculty to perceive the beauty of the natural world.

Again, how can a combination of musical notes, set at different pitches and arranged in a variety of patterns which intermingle with other musical notes, be other than a cacophony? But the ear interprets them as pleasurable, inspiring, tear-jerking, whatever, according to their mood. Someone once said that for him the genius of Bach, Shakespeare and Leonardo da Vinci was enough to prove that God must exist. Even more it is the ability of the human mind to be uplifted by such genius that displays yet more of the glory of God in creation.

To see the power of God in the natural world or to acknowledge that some men and women are touched by God with a genius which seems to be beyond human possibility is to recognise no more than that God acts in his creation. But Moses' experience is that God is more than a puppet-master pulling strings or, better, more than a teacher bringing out the best in his pupils. He is one whose presence is real and active, if not always perceptible in the light of humanity's imperfections and inadequacies.

For a few, the veil is lifted, uniquely, spectacularly. There was the occasion when Jesus took Peter, James and John, his inner core of followers, with him up a mountain to pray. As he prayed, the disciples saw his appearance transfigured, his face shining like the sun and his clothes a dazzling white. Talking with him were two men, Moses and Elijah, who spoke strangely of a 'departure' which was to be accomplished at Jerusalem. Peter and his two companions were full of fear and wonder. And Peter cried out to Jesus, 'Let us make three shrines, one for you, one for Moses and one for Elijah.'

But as he spoke, a bright cloud overshadowed the mountain and a voice from the cloud said, 'This is my beloved Son, with whom I am well pleased. Listen to him.' The disciples fell on their faces in worship and awe, for this was the presence of God. Jesus came over and touched them: 'Rise up. And don't be afraid.' As they looked up, they saw no-one but Jesus alone. 'Tell nobody of the vision you have seen,' Jesus commanded them, 'until the Son of Man has risen from the dead.' (From Matthew 17:1–8.)

A wonder and wonders, a lifting of the veil vouchsafed to but a few; yet could we but see it, God's presence is promised to us for all time and at all times, as surely as it was to Moses. The parting words of Jesus held that promise: 'Lo, I am with you always, to the close of the age' (Matthew 28:20); just as did the assurance which Jesus gave to the disciples shortly before his arrest, that the Counsellor, the Holy Spirit of God, would be with them to guide them into all truth (John 16).

The Christian lives in and with the grace of God to strengthen and uphold. But, as if that were not enough, there is more. It is in an action by God which is both mystery and reality, of which John Henry Newman speaks in his hymn, 'Praise to the Holiest in the height':

> *And that a higher gift than grace*
> *Should flesh and blood refine,*
> *God's presence and his very self,*
> *And essence all divine.*

It is the presence of the Word-made-Flesh in the bread and wine of the Holy Eucharist, the sacramental assurance that He is with us throughout our journey through the wilderness of this world to the promised land of eternal life with Him.

6

Truly Present

Capernaum was a poor little fishing village at the north-western corner of the Sea of Galilee. It held a customs post, where Matthew was the tax-collector (Matthew 9:9), and a small Roman garrison under a centurion. It was also the home of Peter and Andrew, and perhaps because they were his first converts Jesus seems to have made it his base for his ministry in Galilee.

An incident recorded by St Luke (Luke 7:1–10) throws an interesting and unusual light on relations between the Jewish people and the Roman invaders. The centurion had a faithful slave who was seriously ill and sent for the elders of the synagogue to come and heal him. Sometimes in biblical accounts such a request is seen as a threat: 'Heal him – or be punished.' Not so in this case, for the elders at once sent for Jesus, begging him to call and see the centurion.

'He is a good man, worthy to have you do this for him. He loves the Jewish nation and even built our synagogue for us,' they told Jesus. But before Jesus could visit the house, the centurion sent friends to meet him, and to say, 'Lord, please don't trouble yourself to visit, for I am unworthy to receive you under my roof nor to visit you myself. Just say the word, and I know that my servant will be healed. For I too am a man under authority, with soldiers under me. If I say to one, 'Go', he will go; or to another 'Do this', he will do it.'

When Jesus heard this, he marvelled at the centurion's faith.

'I tell you,' he said, 'I have not found such faith, no, not even in Israel.' And when those who had been sent to Jesus returned home, they found the slave had recovered.

It would be in the synagogue built by the centurion, in a village where relations between Jew and Gentile were unusually good, that Jesus preached his most remarkable and controversial sermon, which St John records in great detail (John 6:25–59). But that is to move ahead, for the events which lead up to it have their importance.

It was Jesus' custom from time to time to take his closer disciples away from the clamour of the crowds who gathered wherever they went. It was an opportunity for quiet, for prayer and teaching, all of it in preparation for the task ahead.

On this occasion, just before the feast of the Passover, they had crossed over the northern tip of the Sea of Galilee, from Capernaum up on to the foothills of what we know as the Golan Heights. But they were not to be alone; for the crowds followed, hoping to see more signs and miracles, though the sign they were to see was not of the kind they expected.

Jesus was concerned that the crowds had travelled far and were hungry. 'How much food have we?' he asked his disciples. 'Not enough for these, that's for certain,' Philip replied. A young boy was speaking to Andrew, who told Jesus, 'There is a lad here who has five barley loaves and two small fishes. But they are nothing for a crowd like this.'

'Make them all sit,' ordered Jesus, and the folk, some five thousand of them, sat down on the grass. Jesus took the loaves, gave thanks for them, and distributed them to those who were seated; and the fish too. There was more than enough for all; for when the disciples gathered the left-overs, they filled twelve baskets from the fragments of the barley loaves, abandoned by those who had eaten.

'This is the prophet who is to come into the world!' the people cried when they saw what had been done, and would have taken Jesus and made him king. But he quietly went from them, alone into the hills. By the evening, his disciples went down to the sea to take a boat back to

Capernaum, leaving Jesus in the hills to return by his own means.

The next day, the people who had remained found that Jesus was no longer with them and they too returned to Capernaum, hoping to speak with him again. For had he not, like Moses before him, led them into a wilderness and fed them when they were hungry with bread from heaven? Had not the Lord promised Moses, 'In the morning you shall be filled with bread; then you shall know that I am the Lord your God'? (Exodus 16:12).

> In the morning dew lay round about the camp. And when the dew had gone up, there was on the face of the wilderness a fine, flake-like thing, fine as the hoar-frost upon the ground. When the people of Israel saw it they said, 'What is it?' For they did not know what it was. And Moses said to them, 'It is the bread which the Lord has given you to eat.' (Exodus 16:13–15)

And they gathered each of them just enough for the people in their tent. However much they had gathered, when they had eaten their fill 'he that had gathered much had nothing over, and he that had gathered little had no lack; each gathered according to what he could eat' (Exodus 16:18).

The flight from Egypt under Moses was an event etched into the collective folk-memory of the Jewish people, so it was little wonder that those who shared the bread were quick to make this connection, particularly with the approach of the feast of the Passover. For it was the passing-over by the angel of God of the houses of the children of Israel and the hasty flight from Egypt that the festival recalled.

So, finding him in the synagogue in Capernaum, they asked Jesus, 'Rabbi, when did you come here?'

Jesus replied with a challenge, 'You have come looking for me not because you saw signs but because you ate your fill of the loaves. You are to work, not for food which perishes, but for the food which endures to eternal life, which the Son of Man will give to you.'

'So what must we do, to be doing the works of God?'
they asked.

Jesus replied, 'To believe in him whom God has sent.'

'Then what sign do you do, that we may see and believe
you? Our forefathers ate the manna in the wilderness, as it is
written, "He gave them bread from heaven to eat."'

Jesus said to them, 'I tell you this, it was not Moses who
gave you the bread from heaven; my Father gives you the true
bread from heaven. For the bread of God is that which comes
down from heaven, and gives life to the world.' 'Lord,' they
said, 'give us this bread for ever.'

So far this is a friendly, at times almost light-hearted
discussion, and their response, 'Lord, give us this bread for
ever' is a genuine plea to be given food in the form of the word
of God, teaching which can be taken in to give nourishment
and spiritual sustenance. So far there is no hostility. But for
Jesus, this is too important an opportunity for him not to risk
offending his hearers as he takes the argument forward stage
by stage.

> I am the bread of life; he who comes to me shall not hunger,
> and he who believes in me shall never thirst. But I said to
> you that you have seen me and yet do not believe. All that
> the Father gives me will come to me; and him who comes
> to me I will not cast out. For I have come down from heaven,
> not to do my own will, but the will of him who sent me; and
> this is the will of him who sent me, that I should lose nothing
> of all that he has given me, but raise it up at the last day. For
> this is the will of my Father, that every one who sees the Son
> and believes in him should have eternal life; and I will raise
> him up at the last day. (John 6:35–40)

For some this was already too much, and they muttered
among themselves about it. 'How dare he say, I am the bread
which came down from heaven? Who does he think he is? We
know him, he lodges in our village, some of us know Joseph
and Mary. And now he says, I have come down from heaven.'

Others would suggest that Jesus was speaking in metaphors, that the bread was God's word which had in a sense to be eaten in order to feed and nourish the hearers, that he could indeed say this because he was God's prophet.

Speaking over the growing murmur, Jesus pressed the point further.

'I am the bread of life. Your fathers ate the manna in the wilderness, and they died. This is the bread which comes down from heaven, that a man may eat of it and not die. I am the living bread which came down from heaven; if any one eats of this bread, he will live for ever.' (John 6:48–51)

Even now, there would be those who argued that, yes, he was still speaking in metaphor about the sustenance to be found in taking God's word into oneself. But not with the punch-line that followed.

'I am the living bread which came down from heaven; if any one eats of this bread, he will live for ever; *and the bread which I shall give for the life of the world is my flesh.* (John 6:51)

Now the murmuring had turned into open dispute, and as he continued his teaching in Capernaum's synagogue, he would begin to shout over the uproar. 'How can this man give us his flesh to eat?' 'Do we have to listen to this nonsense?' 'Finish now!' 'Stop him preaching, someone!' But Jesus pressed home his message, over the tumult, knowing its effect and regardless of the support which it lost for him.

'Truly, truly, I say to you, unless you eat the flesh of the Son of man and drink his blood, you have no life in you; he who eats my flesh and drinks my blood has eternal life, and I will raise him up at the last day.

[more noise and shouting]

For my flesh is food indeed, and my blood is drink indeed. He who eats my flesh and drinks my blood abides in me, and I in him.

[the uproar reaches a crescendo and Jesus is almost inaudible]

As the living Father sent me, and I live because of the Father, so he who eats me will live because of me. This is the bread which came down from heaven, not such as the fathers ate and died; he who eats this bread will live for ever.' (John 6:53–8)

Even for many of his own disciples, this was too much, the babblings of a maniac in whom there had seemed so much promise. 'Do you take offence at this?' he asked them. Offence might be taken, but there was no watering down, no leading away from what they might have misunderstood.

After this many of his disciples drew back and no longer went about with him. Jesus said to the twelve, 'Will you also go away?' Simon Peter answered him, 'Lord, to whom shall we go? You have the words of eternal life; and we have believed, and have come to know, that you are the Holy One of God.' (John 6:66–9)

Matthew, Mark and Luke all describe the events of the Last Supper; but for John there is no need. The three tell what was said and done; John explains why it was done and what it means. But he explains it to a Jewish audience who start from where we do not start, with an understanding of food which is alien to our gentile experience.

The food we eat becomes a part of us, our body taking its nourishment and rejecting that which remains. If we did not eat anything, we should at first lose weight and then eventually die. Thus at the Last Supper, as the disciples were eating, 'Jesus took bread, and blessed, and broke it, and gave it to the disciples, and said, "Take, eat; this is my body"' (Matthew 26:26).

If Jesus had taken the broken bread and distributed it with

the words, 'This is your body', it would have seemed almost like an additional grace, another thanksgiving, this time for God's bounty in nourishing our bodies with the food which we eat. But he said instead, 'This is my body.'

Because some animals are unclean to the Jew they may not be eaten, not only for the uncleanness but because to eat such an animal would mean that its uncleanness would become part of the eater. Its impurity would 'become' the eater, and the eater would thus be impure. 'And the Lord said: "These are the living things that you may eat among all the beasts that are on the earth. Whatever parts the hoof and is cloven-footed and chews the cud among the animals, you may eat"' (Leviticus 11:3).

The camel is unclean because although it chews the cud, it does not part the hoof; the pig too because although it parts the hoof and is cloven-footed, it does not chew the cud. Birds of prey such as the eagle, the vulture, the kite and the falcon are unclean, as are 'all that go on their paws, among the animals that go on all fours' (Leviticus 11:27). In general, it is the herbivores that are clean and the carnivores that are unclean, for by eating such an animal the uncleanness which that animal has eaten will be transmitted to the eater, the unclean body becoming part of the eater's body as that body is nourished from it.

But it is the prohibition against blood which underlines the significance of Jesus's words at the Last Supper. 'Only be sure that you do not eat the blood; for the blood is the life, and you shall not eat the life with the flesh' (Deuteronomy 12:23).

The identification of life with blood is understandable if not scientifically accurate. Cut an animal's throat and as the blood ebbs away, so the life ebbs away. In a more primitive age it is not surprising if the assumption were made that blood contains the essence of what is 'life'. If food becomes part of us, more, if in a sense it becomes 'us', then in eating the flesh of an animal from which the blood has not been drained, we take into our very being the 'life' of that animal, whether clean or unclean, so that it becomes part of us. But God has made us above the animal kingdom, as creatures made in God's image with dominion over all other creatures. We must not diminish ourselves by allowing the life of a lesser creature to become 'us'.

In the light of this, the Jewishness of the words said at the Last Supper enables us to hear them in a new light:

> And he took a cup, and when he had given thanks he gave it to them, saying, 'Drink of it, all of you; for this is my blood of the covenant, which is poured out for many for the forgiveness of sins.' (Matthew 26:27–8)

If 'the blood is the life', and if the food we take in becomes 'us', then Jesus is saying, to a people in whose culture this is an essential understanding, 'I am giving you bread which is my body, and wine which is my blood, and in doing so, I am giving you my very life and presence to be with you and, more than that, to be "you".' No wonder then can he preach as he preached to the people of Capernaum in their synagogue:

> 'Truly, truly, I say to you, unless you eat the flesh of the Son of man and drink his blood, you have no life in you; he who eats my flesh and drinks my blood has eternal life, and I will raise him up at the last day. For my flesh is food indeed, and my blood is drink indeed. He who eats my flesh and drinks my blood abides in me, and I in him. As the living Father sent me, and I live because of the Father, so he who eats me will live because of me. This is the bread which came down from heaven, not such as the fathers ate and died; he who eats this bread will live for ever.' (John 6:53–8)

Sadly, just as these words caused offence to many of those who heard Jesus in Capernaum, so that even some of his own disciples went with him no longer, so they have caused offence, controversy and division in Christendom, not least since the Reformation. But they are the words of Jesus himself, part of the sacred canon of Scripture, spoken to a people who would understand as those from another culture find less comprehensible.

They are the words of life from him who is the source of Life, and they encompass the promise of eternal life in him. Moreover, it is his prayer to the Father that we might be one with him as in the divine unity which the Son shares with the Father.

> 'I do not pray for these only, but also for those who believe in me through their word, that they may all be one; even as thou, Father, art in me, and I in thee, that they also may be in us, so that the world may believe that thou hast sent me. The glory which thou hast given to me I have given to them, that they may be one even as we are one, I in them and thou in me, that they may become perfectly one, so that the world may know that thou hast sent me and hast loved them even as thou hast loved me.' (John 17:20–3)

There is the wonder fulfilled of that awesome prospect in the prayer of St Paul, 'that you might be filled with all the fullness of God'. Could there be any greater gift?

But who is this Jesus of Nazareth who claims that his flesh and blood are given for the life of the world?

Jesus who is called Christ

The great God of heaven is come down to earth,
His mother a Virgin, and sinless his birth;
The Father eternal his Father alone:
He sleeps in the manger; he reigns on the throne.
Then let us adore him, and praise his great love:
To save us poor sinners he came from above.

The first verse of that great, but rarely sung, Christmas hymn sums up the paradox, which is the enigma of God incarnate in Jesus Christ. Of all the mysteries of that 'great God of heaven' this is surely the greatest and most incomprehensible. Can I really believe that the Creator of all things, those seen and those beyond sight and human knowledge, could be born into the world He created? Believe, yes; comprehend, no, no, no.

O wonder of wonders, which none can unfold:
The Ancient of days is an hour or two old;
The Maker of all things is made of the earth,
Man is worshipped by angels, and God comes to birth.

It is certainly the claim which St John made in the prologue to his gospel. In creation, God spoke and it was made:

And God said, 'Let there be light'; and there was light. (Genesis 1:3)

God was the Word, and without the Word nothing was made that was made; and in Jesus, the Word became flesh and dwelt among us, full of grace and truth; and we have beheld his glory, glory as of the only Son from the Father. (John 1:14)

This brings us no nearer to understanding, for John's words are truth clothed in poetry and philosophy. To become faith, they need endorsement by one in whom absolute trust can be placed, that is by Jesus himself. The dilemma for those searching for belief is that to place such absolute trust in the words of Jesus is to acknowledge that he is indeed the incarnate Word of God. And such an argument is a logical contradiction, a circular argument.

What then did this Jesus say of himself? He was cautious always of using the title 'Messiah', because as we shall see later the concept of the Christ–Messiah had gathered connotations of earthly rule which were not part of his intention.

But he was to claim a greater title than that of Messiah. The occasion was the feast of Tabernacles and Jesus and his disciples were in Jerusalem. Tabernacles was one of the three great feasts of the Jewish year, with Passover and Pentecost, and was 'the feast of ingathering at the end of the year, when you gather in from the field the fruit of your labour' (Exodus 23:16). It was customary (and is still the custom of an orthodox Jew today) to dwell in booths or tents, as a commemoration of the forty years spent in the wilderness.

Its ritual involved the use of lights and libations of water, ceremonial acts which Jesus used in teaching about himself. On the seventh day of the feast, the 'great day', Jesus stood up in the Temple and proclaimed, '"If any one thirst, let him come to me and drink. He who believes in me, as the scripture has said, 'Out of his heart shall flow rivers of living water'"' (John 7:40).

It was a challenge well understood by his hearers as they saw the ceremonial water poured out. Some said, 'This is the prophet who is to come.' But others said, 'No, this is

the Christ.' 'Don't be foolish – he's a Galilean. Scripture
says that Christ will be descended from David and come
from Bethlehem.' Some wanted him arrested for disturbing
the feast, but no-one laid hands on him.

The Temple police went to the chief priests and Pharisees,
who asked them, 'Why didn't you arrest him?'

They replied, 'No man ever spoke like this man!'

The Pharisees answered angrily, 'Have you too been taken
in by him? Which of us have you found believing in him?
None of us – just this accursed, uneducated crowd.'

Nicodemus, one of their number who had visited Jesus in
secret, asked, 'Do we condemn someone without a hearing?'

The Pharisees turned on him. 'Are you a Galilean too? Tell
us where the Scriptures say a prophet shall rise in Galilee.'

Then Jesus again used the ceremonial of the Feast of
Tabernacles to illuminate his teaching, this time the use of
lights. '"I am the light of the world; he who follows me
will not walk in darkness, but will have the light of life"'
(John 8:12).

By now the Pharisees themselves had come to join battle
with him: 'You are bearing witness to yourself; your testimony
is not true.' In the acrimonious exchange which followed, Jesus
ended with a defence from their own legal system: '"In your
law it is written that the testimony of two men is true; I bear
witness to myself, and the Father who sent me bears witness
to me"' (John 8:17–18).

'Where is your Father?' they challenged, just possibly a
descent to personal abuse with rumours about his origins in
mind, as if to say, 'Oh yes, we know all about your mother.
Wasn't married, was she, when she had you? Who's your real
father? – not old man Joseph for sure!' This may not be so
far-fetched when seen in the light of a further attack a short
time later in the argument.

'Abraham is our father,' the Pharisees said to him. Jesus
replied,

'If you were Abraham's children, you would do what

Abraham did, but now you seek to kill me, a man who has told you the truth which I heard from God; this is not what Abraham did. You do what your father did.' They said to him, 'We were not born of fornication; we have one Father, even God.' (John 8:39–41)

'Gentle Jesus, meek and mild' may be a comfortable Sunday School portrayal of Jesus. One need only read the accounts of his frequent disputes with his enemies to realise it is far from reality. He is a formidable opponent, ready to go on the offensive with all guns blazing.

> 'Why do you not understand what I say? It is because you cannot bear to hear my word. You are of your father the devil, and your will is to do your father's desires. He was a murderer from the beginning, and has nothing to do with the truth, because there is no truth in him. When he lies, he speaks according to his own nature, for he is a liar and the father of lies. But, because I tell you the truth, you do not believe me. He who is of God hears the words of God; the reason why you do not hear them is that you are not of God.' (From John 8:43–7.)

Strong stuff, which in a church assembly or synod would quickly be ruled out of order: but there was more to come, as the attacks from the Pharisees became more abusive. 'Are not we right to say you are not a Jew at all but a Samaritan. And that you have a devil yourself?'

Jesus dismissed this abruptly, 'No, I do not have a demon. But I tell you this, anyone who keeps my word will never see death.'

Scornful laughter now from his enemies: 'That shows you do have a devil! Abraham died, and so did the prophets, yet you say that anyone who keeps your word will not die. Are you trying to say you are greater than Abraham who died? And the prophets died! Who do you claim to be?'

'Who do you claim to be?' It was a direct challenge, made

to him in the Temple; and his answer could not have been expected.

> 'Your father Abraham rejoiced that he was to see my day; he saw it, and was glad.' The Jews then said to him, 'You are not yet fifty years old, and have you seen Abraham?' Jesus said to them, 'Truly, truly, I say to you, *before Abraham was, I am.*' (John 8:56–8)

'Before Abraham was, I am': the ultimate blasphemy, pronounced in the Temple of God itself. The Jewish understanding was that to know someone's name was to have a power over them, for the name revealed the character. So the name of God could never be known, never uttered. When Moses was called by God to lead the children of Israel out of Egyptian slavery to the land which God had promised them, there was one slight difficulty. Moses had left Egypt under a cloud, and was less than popular with his own people. So he voiced the problem and said to God,

> 'Who am I that I should go to Pharoah, and bring the sons of Israel out of Egypt?' He said, 'But I will go with you; and this shall be the sign for you that I have sent you: when you have brought forth the people out of Egypt, you shall serve God upon this mountain.' (Exodus 3:11–12)

Moses was not satisfied. The people would need more proof than something which would happen later. So Moses persisted.

> 'If I come to the people of Israel and say to them, "The God of your fathers has sent me to you," and they ask, "What is his name?" what shall I say to them?' God said to Moses, 'I AM WHO I AM.' And he said, 'Say this to the people of Israel, "I AM has sent me to you."' (Exodus 3:13–14)

The meaning of I AM is irrelevant. All that matters is that

this is the nearest that God came to revealing his name to the children of Israel. So when Jesus says, in the Temple of Jerusalem, the holiest of all places to the Jewish people, 'Before Abraham was, I AM', he is declaring, by the use of a term which to his hearers was unambiguous in its meaning and unmistakable in its intent, that he holds the authority to use the revealed name of God as his own.

No wonder his hearers took up stones to throw at him, for this was the blasphemy of all blasphemies, unforgivable, and punishable only by death. He returned to the theme a short time later, again in the Temple, in the portico of Solomon.

This time it was the winter feast of Dedication, less important than Tabernacles and still observed as *Hanukkah* by modern Jews. Again it involved light, in the lighting of lamps for the worshippers. As Jesus walked, he was surrounded by religious leaders who demanded to know how long he was going to keep them in suspense. 'If you are the Christ, tell us plainly.' Jesus replied that he had told them, but they did not believe his words, nor the evidence of their eyes in the works that he did.

> 'My sheep hear my voice, and I know them, and they follow me; and I shall give them eternal life, and they shall never perish, and no one shall snatch them out of my hand. My Father, who has given them to me, is greater than all, and no one is able to snatch them out of the Father's hand. *I and the Father are one.*' (John 10:27–9)

Again the blasphemy and again they took up stones to stone him. This time there was no easy avenue of escape; so Jesus tried to divert their anger, for now was not the time for the death which was one day to come. 'For which of the good works that I have done do you stone me?' he asked them.

'Not for good works, but for blasphemy. Because you, a man, make yourself God.'

'But in your own scriptures it is written, "I said, you are gods." If he called them gods to whom the word of God came, do you say that I, whom God consecrated and sent into the world, am blaspheming because I said, "I am the Son of God"?'

'If I am not doing the works of my Father, then do not believe me; but if I do them, even though you do not believe me, believe the works, that you may know and understand that *the Father is in me and I am in the Father.*' (John 10:37–8)

Again the blasphemy and again they tried to arrest him, but he escaped from them.

As I consider such extraordinary claims, I am left with three possibilities. He could quite simply be mad, and psychiatrists are by no means unfamiliar with those who claim divinity for themselves; or he could be lying, and in either case, two thousand years of Christian teaching is therefore based on insanity or deceit.

But I know, KNOW, what he has done in my own life and in the lives of countless others, and so I am left only with the third possibility: that all he said and claimed was true, that he is indeed the Word made Flesh, truly God and truly man, the great God of heaven come down to earth, the one in whom 'the whole fullness of deity dwells bodily' (Colossians 2:9).

O wonder of wonders, which none can unfold:
The Ancient of days is an hour or two old;
The Maker of all things is made of the earth,
Man is worshipped by angels, and God comes to birth.
Then let us adore him and praise his great love:
To save us poor sinners he came from above.

8

God's Call – Mary the Maiden

We have an elderly relative who is a brilliant story-teller. Her collections of tales, of recent events like minor operations or sundry other visits to hospital, of major traumas in her life in a varied selection of deaths, of childhood incidents seventy or more years ago, are related as if they happened yesterday. Like a continuous tape, the words never vary and every conversation is repeated without straying from an unwritten text which has served, sometimes for decades, to tell her story. It needs only the mention of a name, a reminder of a date, an association of an event, and the needle will drop into the familiar groove.

My wife once commented, I think facetiously at first but then seriously on the realisation that she had hit a nail on the head, that the old lady's gift was one proof for her that the gospel narratives are true. For these emerged from a generation when story-telling was the means of relating events, with a natural gift honed by a frequency of use which is not in our modern experience. Except for the old lady and a few like her.

Could it be that the birth narratives in the gospels according to Matthew and Luke are a fruit of that different, lost experience? that when Luke (Luke 2:51) records that Mary 'kept all these things in her heart', he is recording the source from which the narratives came? We know that from the cross, Jesus commended his mother into the care of the apostle John:

'Woman, behold, your son!' Then said he to the disciple,

'Behold, your mother!' And from that hour the disciple took her to his own home. (John 19:26–7)

Maybe Mary in her old age would regale visitors and friends with the same stories, over and over, of events in the life of her beloved son, the birth stories among them. 'Do you remember when we ran out of wine at the wedding?' 'Have I ever told you about those strange men who came to us in Bethlehem? And the shepherds?' And the story would begin its familiar course, word for word, as it had a thousand times before, affection and respect hindering the response, 'Well, yes, you have told us – often!'

Perhaps afterwards they would say, 'Mary was on good form yesterday – we had the one about the angel in Nazareth and then she got on to what happened at the inn in Bethlehem.' 'Oh, I had the story of how they left Jesus behind in Jerusalem and found him in the Temple – she always tells me that one!' 'Never changes a word, does she? I've heard them so many times I could tell them myself.' 'Why don't you? Or better, why not write them down with all the other stories about him?'

It may be that this is fanciful, that the birth narratives are no more than legends which have attached themselves to more important (and truer) accounts of Jesus in his ministry and teaching. But it is not as impossible as some scholars suggest that, in an age of story-telling, Mary did tell and re-tell events which were so much a part of her experience.

Historically true or not, there is buried within the narratives an example of God's call and a girl's response which is a pattern for all Christian vocation.

It was in the sixth month of her cousin Elizabeth's pregnancy with the one who would be known as John the Baptist that 'the angel Gabriel was sent from God to a city of Galilee named Nazareth, to a virgin betrothed to a man whose name was Joseph, of the house of David: and the virgin's name was Mary. And he came to her and said, "Hail, O favoured one, the Lord is with you"' (Luke 1:26–28).

It is hardly surprising that this young girl was frightened:

alone, approached by a strange figure and addressed in a peculiar fashion. Was it a madman? Or a rapist? Or just a man making up to a pretty girl? So she 'considered in her mind what sort of greeting this might be. And the angel said to her, "Do not be afraid, Mary, for you have found favour with God. And behold, you will conceive in your womb and bear a son, and you shall call his name Jesus"' (Luke 1:29–31).

Here is God's call, simply stated: that Mary has been chosen to conceive a child who will be called Jesus. But it was not quite so simple, for the angel's words which follow showed that this was no ordinary child but one of whom the prophets had foretold.

'He will be great, and will be called the Son of the
Most High;
and the Lord God will give to him the throne of his
father David,
And he will reign over the house of Jacob for ever;
and of his kingdom there will be no end.' (Luke 1:32–3)

This was none other than the Messiah who was to come, with the angel echoing the words of the prophet Isaiah:

For to us a child is born, to us a son is given;
and the government shall be upon his shoulder,
and his name shall be called, 'Wonderful Counsellor,
Mighty God,
Everlasting Father, Prince of Peace.'
Of the increase of his government and of peace
there will be no end,
upon the throne of David, and over his kingdom,
to establish it, and to uphold it
with justice and with righteousness
from this time forth and for evermore. (Isaiah 9:6–7)

It was an awesome vocation for a young girl, and perhaps the implications did not at first sink in. At any rate, her initial response was a practical one. 'And Mary said to the angel, "How can this be since I have no husband?"' (Luke 1:34).

She was betrothed to Joseph but that is not marriage and they had not come together in intercourse. The angel explained that she would conceive through the power of God, '"Therefore the child to be born will be called holy, the Son of God"' (Luke 1:35).

Cousin Elizabeth had conceived in her old age, and if that could happen Mary could surely see that nothing was impossible with God. But there were other practical worries that must have raced through Mary's young head. What would people say, the neighbours, her friends? Who would believe a story about an angel? And how would she explain to Joseph? or worse still to her mother? What if she were to be accused of adultery? The penalty for that was stoning. All good reasons why she should refuse to accept God's call; as there are almost always reasons why a true vocation should be accepted with hesitancy.

But for Mary, it is God's call and, doubts and problems cast aside, it must be accepted: '"Behold, I am the handmaid of the Lord; let it be to me according to your word"' (Luke 1:38).

There was a time, in Roman Catholic and High Anglican churches, that a devotion called the Angelus was recited at the end of every eucharist. The practice has now almost disappeared, but it did provide a timely reminder about a Christian's vocation. The responses in the Angelus display the call of God, the acceptance, and the result:

The Angel of the Lord brought tidings to Mary:
    And she conceived by the Holy Ghost.

Behold, the handmaid of the Lord:
    Be it unto me according to thy word.

And the Word was made flesh,
    And dwelt among us.

The incarnation was a unique event, a possibility which

ensued from Mary's obedience to God's call, though it was not dependent upon it. Had she declined, God's purpose would not have been thwarted, and we have no means of knowing if others had declined before her.

But that the Word might become flesh did depend on one human being's acceptance of God's call, if not by Mary then by another young woman at a time of God's choosing. Moreover, to accept God's call to a particular work will always result in a kind of incarnation. It will of course never again be the particular incarnation, when the Word became flesh in Jesus Christ, whereby we might behold his glory, the glory as of the only-begotten from the Father, full of grace and truth.

But God does choose to act through us, and our acceptance of His call, be it for something great or something small, of which sometimes we are aware and sometimes not, does mean that He is able to fulfil through us his purpose for the world. When we respond, 'Let it be to me according to your word', then in some way the Word does become flesh and dwell among us.

No-one has summed up the nature of Christian vocation better than the medieval writer of the spiritual classic, *The Cloud of Unknowing*.

Look forward, not backward. See what you lack, not what you have already; for that is the quickest way of getting and keeping humility. Your whole life must now be one of longing, if you are to achieve perfection. And this longing must be in the depths of your will, put there by God, with your consent. But a word of warning: he is a jealous lover, and will brook no rival; he will not work in your will if he does not have sole charge; *he does not ask for help, he asks for you.* (*The Cloud of Unknowing*, Penguin, 1961, p. 52.)

9

God's Call – the Good News and the Bad

Light and more light, brighter than stars and sun and moon; colours more varied than the rainbow, fluorescent and subtle, glowing and pastel; living creatures moving, four of them, all with faces of man and lion and ox and eagle. In their midst more light, burning coals of fire, and lightning, flickering and shooting; light more dazzling than the brightest sun throbbing, bursting, blazing, shimmering. Beneath them wheels, sparkling with precious stones, rising or moving or still, as if with and a part of the creatures. Above the four living creatures, whose wings thundered in flight, was the shining firmament and above that, a throne as blue as sapphire. It was the throne of God and on it in His glory and majesty sat the Creator of all things.

Such was the vision granted to the prophet whose name was 'the Strength of God'.

To know someone's name was to have power over them – or so at least it was understood by the people of the Old Testament, where the name revealed something of the character of the person. Thus when Jacob wrestled with the angel, the angel asked him, 'What is your name?' and he said, 'Jacob' (which means 'He that supplants'). The angel replied,

'Your name shall no more be called Jacob, but Israel (which means "One who wrestles with God"), for you have wrestled with God and with men, and prevailed.' Then Jacob asked

him, 'Tell me, what is your name?' But he said, 'Why is it
that you ask my name?' And there he blessed him. So Jacob
called the place Peniel, saying 'For I have seen God face to
face, and yet my life is preserved.' (Genesis 32:27–30)

There are three Old Testament prophets whose names mean,
in English, the Strength of God, the Exalter of God, and the
Salvation of God. It was to the first of these, whom we know
better as Ezekiel, that there was granted a remarkable vision
from God, in which he saw four beasts and, above them, the
glory of heaven and God enthroned in majesty.

> Such was the appearance of the likeness of the glory of the
> Lord. And when I saw it, I fell upon my face, and heard the
> voice of one speaking. And he said to me, 'Son of man,
> stand upon your feet, and I will speak with you.' And
> when he spoke to me, the Spirit entered into me and set
> me upon my feet and I heard him speaking to me. (Ezekiel
> 1:28–2:22)

God gave Ezekiel a scroll to eat which he found to be 'sweet
as honey' in his mouth as he ate it, and in so doing he accepted
the call which God had given him to preach and prophesy to
the people of Israel. Could a call from God be more powerful
than that? First a vision of the glory of God and then to be
given by God the very words he must speak.

> 'Son of man, get you to the house of Israel, and speak
> with my words to them. For you are not sent to a people
> of foreign speech and a hard language, whose words you
> cannot understand.'

So much for the good news. Now the bad, the sting in
the tail.

> 'But the house of Israel will not listen to you; for they are
> not willing to listen to me; because all the house of Israel are

of a hard forehead and of a stubborn heart. Behold, I have
made your face hard against their faces, and your forehead
hard against their foreheads.'

Yet it is God's call and God's command and Ezekiel must
obey, though they are indeed a rebellious house.

'Son of man, all my words that I speak to you receive in
your heart, and hear with your ears. And go, get you to
the exiles, to your people, and say to them, "Thus says the
Lord God": whether they hear or refuse to hear.' (Ezekiel
3:4–11)

There is no choice, no excuse to be offered, no place for a
request for an easier task. It is the call of God and it must be
obeyed.

So too with Jeremiah, the One who Exalts God, who was
chosen by God even before he was conceived.

'Before I formed you in the womb I knew you,
and before you were born I consecrated you;
I appointed you a prophet to the nations.'

Then I said, 'Ah, Lord God! Behold, I do not know how to
speak, for I am only a youth.' (Jeremiah 1:4–6)

In a true vocation, there is almost always a cause to hesitate.
Not the hesitation which makes for excuses, which says,
'Sorry, Lord, I have other plans.' Rather it is the perplexity
that God has chosen me when He really could have done rather
better. I well recall being asked to let my name go forward for
a senior post which involved a training role. I knew I could do
the job, but at the conference during which I was approached I
felt strongly that another priest present would be much better
suited to the position. But it seemed right that I should allow
the selection process to take its course.

By the time of the interview, I was convinced that it was

not right for me, but protocol in this particular case required that if I were offered the job I had no choice but to accept. I spent a miserable three weeks until the letter arrived regretting that another had been chosen. I was delighted for myself, and delighted as well that the person appointed was the priest I had believed was better suited. But it was right that I allowed the selection process to reject me, rather than that I should have withdrawn on my own initiative.

When the hesitancy arises from a doubt about one's suitability, it may be that God knows better than we do about what He can do with us. So many times in forty years in the ministry have I been faced with a task which on any sensible, rational assessment was quite beyond my capabilities, and always, if it is God's call, He makes up for what is lacking. God never calls us to that which we cannot do, however unlikely or even absurd it might appear to be.

In the case of Mary, the mother of Jesus, when called to bear the Son of God, it was the apparently insuperable difficulty that she had never been with a man. For Jeremiah, it was the modesty which led him to point out his youth.

> But the Lord said to me,
>   'Do not say "I am only a youth";
> for to all to whom I shall send you you shall go,
>   and whatever I command you you shall speak.
> Be not afraid of them,
>   for I am here with you to deliver you, says the Lord.'
> Then the Lord put forth his hand and touched my mouth;
>   and the Lord said to me,
> 'Behold, I have put my words in your mouth.
> See, I have set you this day over nations and over kingdoms,
>   to pluck up and to break down,
>   to destroy and to overthrow,
>   to build and to plant.' (Jeremiah 1:6–10)

What could be better for Jeremiah? Not only to be called by

God but to be assured that he had been chosen even before he was conceived. Not only to be given the very words of God to utter but to be endued with power and strength from God himself by which to fulfil his vocation.

But it was as if God was saying, 'Wait a moment, Jeremiah. That is the good news. Now hear the bad.' A conqueror was to come from the north, and the message which Jeremiah was to give to his people was one of judgment.

> 'I will utter my judgements against them, for all their wickedness in forsaking me; they have burned incense to other Gods, and worshipped the works of their own hands. But you, gird up your loins; arise, and say to them everything that I command you. Do not be dismayed by them, lest I dismay you before them. And behold, I make you this day, a fortified city, an iron pillar, and bronze walls, against the whole land, against the kings of Judah, its princes, its priests, and the people of the land. They will fight against you; but they shall not prevail against you, for I am with you, says the Lord, to deliver you.' (Jeremiah 1:16–19)

It is a hard and dangerous call, but the promise – as always, however difficult and however impossible the call – is that God will be with him to defend him and to deliver him. He has no need of any other weapon.

Isaiah is the one called The Salvation of God. He too had a vision of the glory of God, and its account, one of the most noble in the whole of Scripture, is familiar to most priests of the Church of England as the lesson read at the Ordination Service:

> In the year that king Uzziah died I saw the Lord sitting upon his throne, high and lifted up; and his train filled the temple. Above him stood the seraphim; each had six wings: with two he covered his face, and with two he covered his feet, and with two he flew. And one called to the other and said: 'Holy, holy, holy is the Lord of hosts; the whole earth

is full of his glory.' And the foundations of the thresholds
shook at the voice of him who called, and the house was
filled with smoke. And I said: 'Woe is me! For I am lost;
for I am a man of unclean lips, and I dwell in the midst of
a people of unclean lips; for my eyes have seen the king,
the Lord of hosts!' (Isaiah 6:1–5)

For Jeremiah, the task to which God was calling him seemed
impossible because he was too young; to Mary, the mother of
Jesus, impossible that she should bear a child for the practical
reason that she had not 'been with a man'. Such hesitancy is a
necessary part of our response to God's call. So too is Isaiah's
recognition of his own unworthiness.

It is possible to believe one is called to a task by God and to
feel immediately, 'How wise and sensible He is! I can certainly
do that and indeed am really very worthy to be so called. I
have so much to offer – intelligence, dedication, spirituality, an
easy-mixer and pretty blameless in my behaviour. Yes, Lord,
you've made the right choice this time!' If that is the response
then one can be 99 per cent certain that the call is not from God
but stems from personal conceit, from a spiritual arrogance
which has created a blindness to one's inner weaknesses and
private ambition.

Isaiah has no doubt that he is unworthy; he has been granted
a vision of God's glory yet he is a 'man of unclean lips' who
dwells 'in the midst of a people of unclean lips': 'Woe is me!
For I am lost.' But the Lord removes the difficulty by showing
him that his unworthiness has been purged:

> Then flew one of the seraphim to me, having in his hand
> a burning coal which he had taken with tongs from the
> altar. And he touched my mouth, and said: 'Behold, this
> has touched your lips; your guilt is taken away, and your
> sin forgiven.' (Isaiah 6:6–7)

When a certain bishop was appointed to a senior post in the
Church of England, it was revealed in the press that he had

had a conviction for indecency in a public toilet many years ago. It was an action (the indecency, that is) which was not only criminal but also, in the Church's eyes, sinful. So how could the Church appoint such a man? Was this not one more indication that the Church of England had abandoned moral standards in favour of those of the secular world? Or so the argument went.

It was difficult to convey to critics that the heart of the Christian gospel is repentance, forgiveness and a fresh start. The bishop had not merely received a conviction in the civil court – and would bear with it a feeling of shame for the rest of his life – but had presented himself in sorrow and penitence before the throne of God. The death of Jesus Christ on the cross paid the penalty for all our sins, gave us the promise of a restored relationship with God which we could never deserve, and wiped the slate clean. Of course the bishop was a sinner. But what bishop is not? What priest is not? What Christian is not? If God chooses to call sinners to fulfil his purpose on earth, it is because there is no-one else to call except those who are sinners.

As soon as Isaiah sees that God has restored him by purging his sin, his hesitancy has had the remaining stumbling-block removed:

And I heard the voice of the Lord saying: 'Whom shall I send and who will go for us?' And I said, 'Here am I! Send me.' (Isaiah 6:8)

So the good news: a vision of God's glory, a purging of all sin and unworthiness, a direct call from God which receives a direct response. But once again it is as if the Lord has said, 'Now, Isaiah, you've heard the good news: here is the downside.'

Go and say to this people: 'Hear and hear, but do not understand; see and see, but do not perceive.' Make the heart of this people fat and their ears heavy, and shut their eyes; lest they see with their eyes, and understand with their hearts, and turn and be healed.' (Isaiah 6:9–11)

Isaiah's astonished response to this has almost a scream of despair in it: 'How long, O Lord?' It is one thing to be sent to speak to a people who are a hard-hearted rebellious house as Ezekiel was; or, as Jeremiah, to a people who would fight against a message which would challenge their very nationhood. But to be promised that the Lord himself would deafen the ears of the people and shut their eyes to the very message which he had been called to preach – little wonder that he cried out, 'Lord, how long must I bear this?'

The reality is that when God calls us to any task, he never promises that it will be easy, that the journey will be peaceful or the road without pitfalls. How could this be, when we are called to follow one who bore a cross for our sakes and who expects us to take up a cross for his sake?

Jesus told his disciples, 'If any man would come after me, let him deny himself and take up his cross and follow me. For whoever would save his life will lose it, and whoever loses his life for my sake will find it. For what will it profit a man, if he gains the whole world and forfeits his life?' (Matthew 16:24–6)

In recent years, Isaiah's cry, 'Lord, how long?' has never been far from my own lips as I see the Church I love abandoning or compromising or watering down the truths entrusted to it, turning away from the heritage which has contributed so much that is good to our nation and society. Yet in my heart I know that it was for this very time that God called me – and many other Christians lay and ordained who share this agony – called us to his Church and some to his priesthood often many decades ago.

It is not for us to count the cost, or to understand the reasons, or to expect too soon the Light of God which will in His own time burst forth at the end of the dark tunnel of the present day. Our task is simply to be faithful, faithful to our calling and faithful to the truths which God has revealed in Jesus Christ.

God's answer to Isaiah's cry is uncompromising. How long?

> Until cities lie waste without inhabitant, and houses without men, and the land is utterly desolate, and the Lord removes men far away, and the forsaken places are many in the midst of the land. And though a tenth remain in it, it will be burned again, like a terebinth or an oak, whose stump remains standing when it is felled. (Isaiah 6:11–13)

'The holy seed,' says Isaiah, 'is the stump.' And therein is our hope at the times even of the greatest despair. *The holy seed is the stump.* God's will cannot be thwarted nor his truths destroyed. However weak or insignificant or marginalised or ridiculed, the stump, the remnant that remains, will be the seed from which renewal comes. The powerful and majestic forest can be burnt to a blackened cinder; but its very destruction produces the heat to enliven the dormant seeds which are the new forest that shall be. When the King of Syria surrounded the city of Dothan with a great army, seeking the death of Elisha the prophet, Elisha's servant cried out in fear,

> 'Alas, my master, what shall we do?' Elisha said, 'Fear not, for those who are with us are more than those that are with them.' Then Elisha prayed, and said, 'O Lord, I pray, open his eyes that he may see.' So the Lord opened the eyes of the young man, and he saw; and behold, the mountain was full of horses and chariots of fire around Elisha. (2 Kings 6:15–17)

Those who are called of God to whatever task need not fear their inadequacy, nor the power of those who oppose them, nor the trials which may beset them in sharing the burden of Christ's cross. It is God's call and God's church and He must prevail.

For consider your call, brethren; not many of you were wise according to worldly standards, not many were powerful, not many were of noble birth; but God chose what is foolish in the world to shame the wise, God chose what is weak in the world to shame the strong, God chose what is low and despised in the world, even things that are not, to bring to nothing things that are, so that no human being might boast in the presence of God. He is the source of your life in Christ Jesus, whom God made our wisdom, our righteousness and sanctification and redemption. (1 Corinthians 1:26–30)

10

John the Baptiser
or
Expect the Unexpected

There can surely be no parish priest, no minister of the gospel, no-one engaged in the work of the Church, for whom the words of Jesus do not ring a bell when he asked:

> To what shall I compare this generation? It is like children sitting in the market-places and calling to their playmates, 'We piped to you, and you did not dance; we wailed, and you did not mourn.' For John came neither eating nor drinking, and they say, 'He has a demon'; the Son of man came eating and drinking, and they say, 'Behold, a glutton and a drunkard, a friend of tax-collectors and sinners.' (Matthew 11:16–19)

There are always one or two in every congregation – and more than that in some – who believe that God has called them to be a thorn in the vicar's flesh. A deeply-committed Christian thorn, of course, who will end the most unpleasant of missives with the words: 'In Christian love, from your brother (sister) in Christ.' It is a cross to be borne with fortitude and resignation, and it is a comfort to know that we share it with John the Baptist and Jesus himself.

John was a prophet in the tradition of the most fiery

of Old Testament wayside preachers, and to some of his hearers he would have been no more than a comedy turn. He ranted against sin, even the sins of King Herod, cutting an astonishing, even fearsome, figure in 'garment of camel's hair, and a leather girdle around his waist'. His message was uncompromising and he was fearless in the fulfilment of the task which God had given him. He made converts, but not at any price:

> When he saw many of the Pharisees and Sadducees coming for baptism, he said to them, 'You brood of vipers! Who warned you to flee from the wrath to come? Bear fruit that befits repentance, and do not presume to say to yourselves, "We have Abraham for our father"; for I tell you, God is able from these stones to raise up children to Abraham.' (Matthew 3:7–9)

But those who saw beyond the outward voice of the prophet were touched in their hearts by the voice of God. They saw their sins and their sinfulness and were moved to repent and be baptised; but it was no more than a first step, a preparation along the way. As John told them, 'I baptise with water for repentance, but he who is coming is mightier than I, whose sandals I am not worthy to carry; he will baptise you with Holy Spirit and with fire' (Matthew 3:11).

They were to expect the unexpected: indeed at the heart of the story of John the Baptist, there is always the warning that things will not be as they seem. At his beginning there is the unexpected promise of a son to the elderly Zechariah and Elizabeth, and not of an ordinary child but of one who will be great before the Lord, who 'will turn many of the sons of Israel to the Lord their God', who 'will go before him in the power and spirit of Elijah', who will 'make ready for the Lord a people prepared'. (From Luke 1:15–17.)

As always with God's call, as with Ezekiel, Jeremiah, Isaiah, as even with Mary, there was hesitation, a difficulty to be overcome when the angel brought the news to Zechariah:

'How shall I know this? For I am an old man, and my wife is advanced in years.' And the angel answered him, 'I am Gabriel, and I stand in the presence of God; and I was sent to speak to you, and to bring you this good news.' (Luke 1:18–19)

There was to be no argument: it was God's decision, God's call, and what is to be will be. For his scepticism, Zechariah was struck dumb by the angel. Again there is the unexpected at the child's circumcision and naming, when those gathered would have called him Zechariah after his father.

But his mother said, 'Not so; he shall be called John.' And they said to her, 'None of your kindred is called by this name.' And they made signs to his father, inquiring what he would have him called. And he asked for a writing tablet, and wrote, 'His name is John.' And they all marvelled. (Luke 1:59–63)

John is the chosen one who is to prepare the way for the Messiah, the 'voice of one crying in the wilderness' (Isaiah 40:3; Matthew 3:3); and he prepared his own disciples for the day when they must leave him and follow the one who is truly the Way. The two mothers, Elizabeth and Mary, were cousins and it is inconceivable that John did not know, or at least know of, his kinsman Jesus of Nazareth. But it is at a dramatic and unexpected moment in Bethany-beyond-Jordan, where John had been baptising, that the realisation suddenly came upon him that the one for whom he was called to prepare the way was none other than that same Jesus, son of cousin Mary. 'Look there,' he told his followers, 'that is the man, that is the Lamb of God who will take away the sins of the world.' It is a moment for awe and wonder.

This is he of whom I said, 'After me comes a man who ranks before me, for he was before me.' I myself did not know him; but for this I came baptising with water, that he might be revealed to Israel.' (John 1:30–1)

As John's followers begin to leave to serve the One for whom the way was prepared, there is again the unexpected, at least for Nathanael of Cana-in-Galilee. The village of Cana-in-Galilee lies nearby the city of Nazareth, some five miles along the road to Tiberias, perhaps with pretensions to being rather up-market – a desirable place to move out to when prosperous enough to make the daily journey into the city. With excitement in his voice, Philip wanted to share his discovery of Jesus with Nathanael.

'We have found him of whom Moses in the law and also the prophets wrote, Jesus of Nazareth, the son of Joseph.' Nathanael said to him, 'Can anything good come out of Nazareth?' Philip said to him, 'Come and see.' (John 1:45–6)

Jesus welcomed him with the words, 'Behold, an Israelite indeed, in whom is no guile!' But how can Jesus know him, Nathanael wondered. 'Before Philip spoke to you, I saw you under the fig-tree.'

'Rabbi, you are the Son of God! You are the king of Israel!' Nathanael's over-the-top response must have brought a smile to the face of Jesus: 'Because I said I saw you under the fig-tree is that enough to make you believe? You'll see greater things than that!'

If there had been the unexpected here for Nathanael, there was infinitely more to come: '"Truly, truly, I say to you, you will see heaven opened, and the angels of God ascending and descending upon the Son of man"' (John 1:51).

Yet lying in prison, doubts began to assail John. Was Jesus really the Messiah? Had he made a mistake, pointed out the wrong one, been taken in by the undoubted godliness of his kinsman, a godliness which he might not have noticed in a stranger? Was not the Messiah to be one who would lead the people of Israel like a great army against the pagan Roman army of occupation and set up a kingdom with God Himself at its head? John heard much in prison of the doings of Jesus, but nothing of this declaration of messiahship. So the followers who remained with him were sent to Jesus to ask, 'Are you really the one who is to come, or should we be looking for another?'

And Jesus answered them, 'Go and tell John what you hear and see: the blind receive their sight and the lame walk, lepers are cleansed and the deaf hear, and the dead are raised up, and the poor have the good news preached to them. And blessed is he who takes no offence at me.' (Matthew 11:4–6)

This is more than a call to look for the evidence of their own eyes. It is a rebuke to John, so ready to proclaim himself – and rightly so – to be the fulfilment of Isaiah's prophecy of a voice crying in the wilderness, Prepare the way of the Lord. He must as well see the truth of other words of Isaiah in his promise of the coming Messiah: 'Then the eyes of the blind shall be opened, and the ears of the deaf unstopped; then shall the lame man leap like a hart, and the tongue of the dumb sing for joy' (Isaiah 35:5–6).

To expect the unexpected is a constant theme in Scripture, not merely in the unexpected nature of God's call nor in its often unexpected out-working. It is there in our seeking of God's presence and God's comfort. When Elijah fled from the wrath of Jezebel, he had pleaded in his depression that he might die: 'It is enough; now, O Lord, take away my life; for I am no better than my fathers.' After fulfilling God's will, all had forsaken him and fled: 'I, even I only, am left; and they seek my life, to take it away.' He was called to stand upon the mount before the Lord:

And behold, the Lord passed by, and a great and strong wind rent the mountains, and broke in pieces the rocks before the

Lord, but the Lord was not in the wind; and after the wind
an earthquake, but the Lord was not in the earthquake; and
after the earthquake a fire, but the Lord was not in the fire;
and after the fire a still small voice. (1 Kings 19:11–12)

Many years ago when I was vicar of a parish on the edge
of London, a family arrived and joined our worshipping
community. The husband, a senior doctor, explained to me,
kindly, that God had called them to come to us so that we
might have the Holy Spirit in our midst. I commented that
they were very welcome but that I believed the Holy Spirit
was already with us. And privately I thought his own call
to come to us was from his own arrogance rather than from
a divine source.

But we did have an Anglican reserve and certainly lacked
the flamboyance of the kind of charismatic worship to which
he was accustomed. After eighteen months he had the humility
to admit to me that he now realised that in spite of our reserve,
we did indeed have the Holy Spirit. The truth is that it is not
for any of us to question another's way of worshipping God,
of expressing the joy of knowing and meeting the living Lord
in Jesus Christ, whatever may be the liturgical equivalent of
the wind, the earthquake, the fire, or the still small voice.

I love the Book of Common Prayer, but I am not put out
by the less formal language of the Alternative Service Book,
worshipping to the accompaniment of guitars and fine hymns
from *Mission Praise*. I can be carried to the gates of heaven
at a cathedral Eucharist in a glorious medieval building; and if
there is an orchestra and a Mozart Mass or an unaccompanied
choir singing Byrd's *Mass for Five Voices*, I can know the
presence of God. But He is there too in the unexpected, if we
look for Him.

When I was vicar of Eaton Bray, a country parish in
Bedfordshire with a beautiful, thirteenth century church, the
delayed installation of a new heating system meant that we
were forced to worship over Christmas in a dilapidated church
hall even then awaiting demolition. It would not, I thought, be

the same. No soft stone lit by candles, no subdued lighting illuminating carvings and arches and columns, none of that subtle feeling which comes of worshipping in a building consecrated by seven centuries of prayer.

I could not have been more mistaken. To hide an ugly metal support in the centre of the hall, we set the altar there; to avoid the depressing sight of dirty peeling walls, we placed the old chairs in a circle around the altar. And the unexpected happened: we were in the stable with the Holy Child of Bethlehem and never had a Christmas been more memorable.

But it is not only in our encounter with God in our worship that we must expect the unexpected. When the father of a boy suffering from fits brought him to Jesus, he begged for help. 'If you can do anything for him, have pity on us and help us.'

And Jesus said, 'If you can! All things are possible to him who believes.' Immediately the father of the child cried out and said, 'I believe; help my unbelief.' (Mark 9:23–4)

At the time when the charismatic doctor came to worship in my parish, I was suffering periodic bouts of migraine. One day, I apologised to him that I had not been able to chair a meeting in his house, explaining that I had had an attack of migraine which had temporarily laid me low. When he asked me what I was doing about it, I took this to be a medical question and described the tablets I had been prescribed.

'Oh, I don't mean that,' he replied. 'Have you asked the Lord to take it away?' I muttered something about the Lord having better things to think about than my migraine, and that anyway Paul had had his thorn in the flesh to keep him from being too proud. He was not impressed.

A week later I had the worst migraine I had ever suffered and in desperation but in total lack of faith, I prayed, 'Come on, Lord, your friend says you can take this away. What about it?' Within three hours it had gone, and I have not had a migraine since. I am ashamed to say I could not bring myself to tell the charismatic doctor. I remain as sceptical now as I was then that this had been a miracle of divine intervention. The next story I have no doubt tells of God's working in healing the whole person. Whether it involved a miracle which defied nature or merely one in which God acted within the natural law, I do not know. But I do know that God acted.

A few months before my ordination in 1955, my mother was diagnosed as having a tumour on the brain. She was anointed with holy oil and we prayed earnestly for her, though again not with too much expectation of healing. After one operation to relieve the pressure, she had further surgery to explore possibilities. The consultant explained afterwards what happened: 'The operation involved boring two holes at the base of the skull and inserting an instrument rather like a knitting needle. As I probed, I suddenly realised I was touching, not the brain, but the tumour itself, and so I removed it. X-rays had showed the tumour right inside the brain and somehow it had moved out to where I found it.'

He paused and then continued, 'I am not a Christian, but I know how you will regard this. I simply have no explanation, for I would have said that this just could not have happened.' A miracle? or something with an as yet unknown medical rationale? Whatever the case, I am sure it was God at work, and the certain miracle was that she died (as indeed she did some seven months later, and from the illness) in the peace of God. Her priest said he felt those last extra months were some of the most fruitful of her life. Healing is not only of the body and we must be ready for the unexpected.

There is the unexpected too in God's forgiveness. The prodigal son in the parable (Luke 15:11–32) is ready with a half-baked excuse and half-sincere penitence for his misdeeds as he returns to the comfort of his family home. But his father brushes away the well-rehearsed apology as he rushes out to meet his son while the lad is 'yet a great way off' (Luke 15:20 AV). 'But while he was yet at a distance, his father saw him and had compassion, and ran and embraced him and kissed him' (Luke 15:20).

God's amazing and unexpected love for the sinner is worth a chapter to itself (see chapter 12).

Jesus points to the unexpected in other parables too. When Jesus was asked by the lawyer, 'Who is my neighbour?', he gave his answer in the parable of the Good Samaritan (Luke 10:25–37). The man travelling from Jerusalem to Jericho fell among thieves who left him for dead. A priest and a Levite saw him lying there and passed by on the other side. It was the Samaritan who took pity on him, binding his wounds and paying for him to stay at an inn until he had fully recovered.

> 'Which of these three, do you think,' Jesus asked the lawyer, 'proved neighbour to the man who fell among robbers?' He said, 'The one who showed mercy on him.' And Jesus said to him, 'Go and do likewise.' (Luke 10:36–7)

Jesus had come to the parable from the lawyer's initial question, put to Jesus to test him, 'Teacher, what shall I do to inherit eternal life?' Jesus turned the question back on him, asking the lawyer,

> 'What is written in the law? How do you read?' And he answered, 'You shall love the Lord your God with all your heart, and with all your soul, and with all your strength, and with all your mind; and your neighbour as yourself.' And he said to him, 'You have answered right; do this, and you will live.' (Luke 10:26–8)

But the lawyer was not satisfied, and 'desiring to justify himself' asked the further question, 'And who is my neighbour?' He could not accept the implications of the answer which Jesus gave to him in the parable. After all, the priest and the Levite were both men of the cloth and were to be respected as keepers of the law. It would be unthinkable that they would fail to put the law into practice by ignoring the needs of the injured man. The third man was a Samaritan, hated by the Jews, particularly the religious leaders, as the representative of a people who had allowed the purity of Judaism to be sullied by foreign influences.

In his answer to the question put to him by Jesus, 'Which of the three was neighbour to the man who fell among thieves?', the lawyer cannot bring himself to say, 'The Samaritan' and instead answers, grudgingly, 'The one who showed mercy on him.' He cannot accept the unexpected possibility that a Samaritan would behave in this way – or, more important for himself, that he must show love and respect for his own Samaritan neighbour.

During the apartheid years in South Africa, I was severely taken to task by leading churchmen involved in the theological and political fight against this evil by which a whole people were oppressed in that country when I delivered a *Thought for the Day* on BBC Radio 4's *Today* programme in which I translated the story into a modern parable.

Early one morning, a young black civil servant was walking from his home in Soweto to work in Johannesburg when he was set upon by a gang of muggers who robbed him, beat him, and left him for dead in the gutter. A little later, a priest saw him and wondered if he should help. But he was already late for an important meeting in the city with clergy of many denominations who were united in fighting against apartheid. It was a busy road and someone else was sure to come by soon to help the man. So he passed quickly by on the other side.

Soon afterwards, a white social worker was driving into Soweto to work at the clinic which had been set up to help those suffering oppression under the cruel regime and already she knew that the queues would be long. And anyway if she did stop, she too might be in danger from muggers. So she drove on, certain that someone else would soon be by to help.

A police patrol car soon drove by, and, seeing the body at the side of the road, the driver stopped and, with his colleague, got out to look. 'Another drunken *kaffir*,' said the older policeman. 'No,' said the younger, 'I think he's injured.' They examined him and realised he was badly injured; and they knew that without help, he would soon die. They radioed for an ambulance, and in the meantime bound his wounds as best they could from their first aid kit. They had discovered where he lived, and when the ambulance had taken him to hospital, they drove into Soweto to let the young man's family know his predicament.

White policemen helping an injured black man? This, I was assured, simply would not happen. Why, it would be laughable if it were not such a political distortion. I should be ashamed as a Christian priest for my racist attitudes and be removed from the rota of contributors for broadcasting propaganda on behalf of the South African Government. Yet if we wish to know the answer to the question 'Who was neighbour to the man who fell among thieves?', we need to put there the one whom for us it could not possibly be, the one whom we *know* would not behave like that.

As always, be it in his call to us, in the mission or witness he requires of us, or in the teaching he offers to us, Jesus makes us face the utterly unexpected.

11

A Meditation

God has created me to do Him some definite service
    He has not committed to another.
I have a mission – I may never know it in this life,
    but I think I shall be told it in the next.
I am a link in a chain,
    a bond of connection between persons.
He has not created me for naught.
I shall do good, I shall be an angel of peace,
    a preacher of truth in my own place
    while not intending it
  – if I do but keep his commandments.

Therefore I will trust him.
Whatever, wherever I am.
If I am in sickness,
    my sickness may serve Him;
If I am in perplexity,
    my perplexity may serve Him;
If I am in sorrow,
    my sorrow may serve Him.
He does nothing in vain.
He knows what He is about.
He may take away my friends,
He may throw me among strangers,

He may make me desolate, make my spirits sink,
  hide my future from me,
– still, He knows what He is about.

John Henry Newman

12

Faith and Grace

In 1958, three years after ordination, I was invited to Sweden to spend a holiday with the warden of a students' hostel at Lund University. He was Pastor Sven-Oscar Berglund, we became immediate friends and our two families have remained so for nearly forty years. During my stay, I had a brief meeting with a retired bishop and theologian, Gustav Aulén, whose book on the atonement, *Christus Victor*, I had dipped into while at seminary. I decided I ought to read it properly and nothing has had so great and immediate an effect on my faith.

In it he sets out three views of the atonement. The first, which he calls the objective or Catholic view, sees the sacrifice of Christ on the cross in the terms of Mrs Alexander's Good Friday hymn: 'There was no other good enough to pay the price of sin.' Because of the sins of mankind, all humanity has been cut off from God. It is a break which only man himself can repair; but man because of sin is incapable of so doing. So the perfect man must come into the world, in the person of Jesus Christ, 'to pay the price of sin' – the substitute sacrifice made by man to God.

This, he suggests, is inadequate, since its effectiveness depends not upon the divine but on the human. Jesus is God, the Word made flesh, but it is in his humanity and not in his divinity that he dies on the cross to save us from our sins.

Then there is the subjective or liberal Protestant view that Jesus is simply an example for us to follow. Insofar as we

follow his example, we become like him and so come nearer
to God's purpose for us. Again it is by man's action and not
God's by which we are brought salvation, that we are enabled
to become at one with Him.

Only in the third view, which he, Aulén, calls the classical
(and not surprisingly, the Lutheran), is the truth to be found
– summed up in the phrase from St Paul, 'God was in
Christ, reconciling the world to himself, not counting their
trespasses against them, and entrusting to us the message of
reconciliation' (2 Corinthians 5:19).

Certainly I had always felt the subjective view to be
unsatisfactory and inadequate, but I had preached sermons
on the substitution view more than once. And I had always
believed that when I fell into sin, I must, with the help of
God's grace, try, try and try again.

Suddenly I saw in a blinding flash that this was totally
inadequate. 'By grace you have been saved, through faith;
and this is not your own doing, it is the gift of God'
(Ephesians 2:8).

God accepts me as I am, warts and all, for that is the nature
of the love of Him who is Love itself. All that is required of
me is to put my trust in His love, to say, 'Help me, for I cannot
manage on my own – the journey is too great for me.' Then and
only then is He able to lift me up into the joy of His presence
and His glory; my sins are not merely forgiven but wiped off
the record, and I can, in St Paul's marvellous words, 'be filled
with all the fullness of God' (Ephesians 3:19). It is His action
and His alone.

It transformed my Christian experience, so that the doctrine
of justification by faith became, together with the conviction
that in the blessed sacrament of Holy Communion one meets
and receives the Real Presence of Jesus, one of the twin
pillars of my life in Christ – the one strongly Catholic
and the other strongly Protestant. Both were the gift of
God, and neither could be earned or deserved. From then
on, as I read the Old Testament I realised that this was
precisely the outworking of the relationship between God

and His chosen people, the children of Israel, at every point in the story.

Read it in a modern parable, just about recognisable as the parable of the Prodigal Son (Luke 15:11–32).

A certain man had two sons, Shimon and Yakob. The younger, Shimon, was resentful of the way his father treated him, ever critical, apparently ungenerous, and one day he asked to be given his share of the family fortune. His father tried to argue: 'Can't you wait until I die? You'll waste it all if I give it to you now.'

'No, I won't,' the son replied. 'But what I will do is to show you that I am just as capable as my brother, that in a few years I'm a good enough businessman to make it into another fortune.' So his father tried another route: 'What about your mother? It will kill her if you leave. Why can't you find a nice Jewish girl to marry? Settle down, raise sons of your own. Be like Yakob.'

But the boy was adamant: he had had enough and he was determined to leave. So his father gave him a large sum of money and he went to a far country. At first he genuinely planned to set up a business, even thought out what it would be. But first, just a bit of excitement – a nice flat, get some expensive transport, join an exclusive club, something to attract friends in a strange country. And the friends came, and the women, and Shimon developed expensive tastes in entertainment, in heavy gambling, excessive in every way that his new friends encouraged him.

He soon realised the money was now much less than his father had given him. But there was still enough, even if the business would not be quite so big and the fortune would take longer to make. Just another six months' pleasure, then another three, then another one, then the money was gone. With it went the women, the friends, the lifestyle. He was penniless, jobless, friendless and a long way from home in a strange country.

Hungry, Shimon tried for this job and that, but he was

homeless, scruffy and a bad risk all round. In the end, in despair, he took work with a pig farmer, ill-paid and only able to afford to eat what the pigs had left of their own meal. Pigs, the unclean animal, untouchable and uneatable for a good Jew.

Then he had an inspiration. 'What a fool I am!' he said to himself. 'My father's servants are better off than I am. He's a good man – and a soft touch. I know what I'll do – I'll go home and say to him, 'Father, I've sinned against heaven (must put that in – he's always at the synagogue) and against you. I'm no longer worthy to be your son, I know, but please give me a job and I'll work as one of your servants.' So he began the long hard journey home, practising all the time his set speech of half-apology.

So far so good: he has turned his back on the good-for-nothing life which he had been leading and he is returning home to the better values of his family. That is not to say he is sorry for the way he has behaved, and that given another slice of the family fortune he would not return at once to the far country to begin again where he had left off. He is sorry for the mess he is in, and little more than that. And human justice and human compassion seem to demand that the story should continue something like this:

When Shimon was still a great way from home, his father's manager saw him and told his employer, 'It looks as if that son of yours is on his way back. I expect he's broke. What do you want me to do? Shall I send him on his way?' Shimon's father was angry and a little sad at his manager's harshness.

'Whatever he's done, Shimon is still my son. Let him in the house and show him to my office. But keep him guessing – don't make him too welcome,' ordered the father. The manager did just that and eventually, after an anxious wait outside the door, Shimon was invited into the office.

For a moment the father kept his head down, writing.

Finally he put down his pen, looked his son firmly in the eyes. 'So what have you to say for yourself?'

'Father,' said Shimon, 'I know I have been a fool. I have sinned against heaven and before you and I'm no longer worthy to be called your son. But please give me a job and I'll work very hard as one of your servants.' By now he had practised the little speech so many times that even to Shimon it sounded weak and inadequate.

His father smiled. 'Of course I'll give you a job. You're my son and I love you. What sort of a father would turn his son away? And I'll tell you this, that if you work hard, you could reach the highest position in the firm if you're the best at the job – but no favouritism, mind! What you've done, the money you've wasted, the sins you've committed, I won't hold any of it against you.'

Shimon wept at his father's kindness, and even his brother Yakob was pleased: 'Shimon, Shimon,' he said, 'are we not fortunate to have so good a father, who forgives us for whatever we do?'

But in fact that is not how the story of the Prodigal Son ends; and St Paul does not speak of faith, hope and niceness ('and the greatest of these is niceness') but of love, which is a much harder taskmaster. For what really happened to the son as Jesus told the story was this:

While Shimon was still a great way from home, his father saw him in the far distance and rushed to meet him where he was. Shimon managed only to get out the first part of his half-hearted excuse, and the father brushed it aside as he organised the welcome for his son who was lost and is found, dead and is alive.

'You go quickly and get a coat for him, clean clothes, shoes for his feet – anything he needs. And you, go and get food – yes, kill the fatted calf, we'll give him a meal to remember.'

Yakob, his elder brother, was not pleased – in fact

he was very angry. 'Why are you doing this for your good-for-nothing son? I've served you faithfully all these years, never putting a foot wrong, never wasting your money, never chasing other women. When did you show me this kind of love?'

'When did I show you my love, Yakob? Why, all the time. But you were always trying so hard to make me love you that you could never see it.'

And that is the point: we simply do not need to try to earn the love of God. The danger is that we almost imagine a ladder set between us and the Father. We clamber up a few rungs and because, by reason of the failings in our humanity, we quickly fall to the bottom again, we say, 'Sorry, God. Please forgive me and I'll try harder next time.' And the more we try, the harder we fall.

The difficult lesson to learn is that it is only when we acknowledge not only our sin but our weakness too, when we say, 'Sorry, Lord, I can't do it on my own but only with your help' that He is able to lift us to Himself, restored, redeemed, sanctified. We are then, as St Paul says, 'accepted in the beloved' (Ephesians 1:6 AV). For the fact is that God accepts us as we are and where we are, not because this good act is balanced against that bad one, not because by our good works we have wormed our way into his favour.

The younger son, Shimon, practised his little speech to please his father but it was brushed aside as the father met him while he was still a great way off – even though the young man was more sorry for himself than for the sins he had committed, ready if given half a chance to do it all again, and perhaps not even aware of the hurt that some of his actions had given his father.

St Paul's great phrase, 'By grace you are saved through faith: it is the gift of God' (Ephesians 2:8), is the heart of the Christian message – that God restores us to a right relationship with himself, a relationship broken by sin, that he will maintain that relationship, if only we ask, by the grace he offers to us, and that this is not for any good works on our part but simply because we have the faith to seek it and the trust that it will be given. It is God's free gift. It can be rejected; but it cannot be bought.

It means that Jesus could declare to the thief dying next to him on another cross, 'Today you will be with me in paradise.' Here was a man who had admitted that he was receiving no less than his crimes deserved, yet who in the excruciating pain of his execution showed a little act of kindness to the innocent Jesus dying next to him: 'Here, mate, you remember me when you come into that kingdom you've been going on about!' The answer was more than he could have bargained for: 'Truly I say to you, today you will be with me in paradise' (Luke 23:43). Paradise? After all his evil deeds? For no more than a kind word? Well, that was what the man said. In human terms, unfair. But the justice of God's love is always beyond question.

The light of love which Jesus detects in the penitent thief on the cross is faint and dim, hardly able to overcome the darkness surrounding it. But it is enough, as it was for the woman taken in adultery in the abject terror of what she thought was to come, as it was for the paralysed man brought to Jesus on a stretcher whom he ordered, 'Rise, take up your bed and walk; your sins are forgiven' (Matthew 9:6), as it was for the young man whose father met him in love while he was 'still a great way off'.

That the love of the father comes while the sinner is 'still a great way off' is a recognition not only that everyone falls far short of the perfection demanded by God but also that part of the imperfection is that we are unable often to recognise the reality of where we have fallen short. The gift of God is not merely that we are accepted at the point at which we acknowledge we can only succeed in his strength rather than our own: it is also that we are accepted even for the sins and failures of which we are not even aware.

Moreover, the sins are not just forgiven but remitted, and one of the weaknesses of the eucharistic prayers in the Alternative

Service Book is that, unlike the Book of Common Prayer which uses the phrase 'remission of our sins', they speak of the blood of Jesus 'shed for you and for many for the forgiveness of sins'. Forgiveness is a human act which says in effect: 'You have hurt me by your unkind words or wicked action, and neither of us can undo what has been done. But I will put it out of my mind and behave as if it has never happened.'

Remission on the other hand is a divine accomplishment by which the sin is removed as if it had never been. Forgiveness writes the word 'SIN' and crosses it out; remission wipes the slate clean.

This is so clearly the message of the gospel of Jesus Christ, the good news which offers hope to all, that it is difficult to comprehend the blindness of those who seek always to minimise or even remove the reality of sin. One modern theologian wrote recently of the 'orgy of monstrously masochistic self-denigration' with which Christian worship is riddled, constantly demanding the confessions of sins rather than rejoicing at human good, sneering at what he described as the 'celestial rescue operation performed through Jesus which is proclaimed as having put things right' (H. Dawes, *Freeing the Faith*, SPCK, 1992).

There was once a phrase, which I understand is now unfortunately omitted, in the Bidding Prayer which opens the Festival of Nine Lessons and Carols broadcast each Christmas from King's College Chapel, Cambridge, which invites us to remember 'all those who know not the Lord Jesus, or who love him not, *or who by sin have grieved his heart of love*'.

When by sin we fall short of God's ideal, we 'grieve his heart of love' and there is the need to put that right. The fundamental point which those who reject the traditional faith altogether overlook is that in admitting our failures before God in worship we simply do not have to indulge in 'an orgy of monstrously masochistic self-denigration' or anything which approaches it. To confess one's sins is for the Christian not to grovel before an unforgiving, demanding deity requiring his pound of flesh, but the most joyful recognition of an acceptance offered by a God who is Love itself.

Yet even where a more moderate stance is taken, it does seem to be the fashion to wish to diminish a sense of sin. The damaging effect of all this is to transfer the responsibility for wrongdoing from the individual to society or 'the government' or 'the system'.

This is precisely the sin of Adam and Eve in the Genesis story (Genesis 3). God tells them they may eat of the fruit of all the trees in the Garden, save that of the tree in the midst of the Garden. The serpent tempts Eve by suggesting God has lied: 'Has God told you that you will die? You will not die. What will happen is that you will be like gods knowing the difference between good and evil.' So the woman eats the fruit and gives her husband the fruit to eat as well.

When they hide from the Lord God, he realises what they have done: 'Have you eaten of the fruit of the tree which I forbade you to eat?' 'Actually, it was my wife's fault,' Adam replies lamely. And, more aggressively, he turns on God: 'In fact, it was the woman *you* gave me, so it's your fault too. Don't try to blame me.' Eve simply pins the fault on the serpent who tempted her.

It is this human characteristic of refusing to accept responsibility for one's own actions that marks the modern attitude to sin adopted by some who would profess and call themselves Christian, but they overturn scriptural teaching from the very first pages of the Bible. It is the root of a deep malaise within our society, and save for the fact that God's truth in the end always wins, it could be a cause for pessimism for the future of the Church. For it would destroy the heart of the Gospel.

Sin cannot be written off as an out-dated concept, nor can we pass on responsibility for our own sins to another. But there is another danger: that we so minimise its importance that we fail to condemn it, in ourselves or in others. By God's grace and God's grace alone, it can be conquered; and by our faith and trust in His love we can be redeemed for Him. His love cannot be quantified or limited. Shakespeare described it perfectly, as if it were God rather than Romeo who speaks:

> My bounty is as boundless as the sea,
> My love as deep; the more I give to thee,
> The more I have, for both are infinite.
> *(Romeo and Juliet*, II. ii. 133)

13

Judgment and Love

'Forgive us our trespasses, as we forgive those who trespass against us': it is a conditional request for forgiveness. We are only able to ask his forgiveness in the same measure that we are able to forgive others for the manner in which they have offended us. That is fair; for how could we expect God's forgiveness when we ourselves are unforgiving?

Jesus explained this in the form of a parable. Peter had asked the question, 'How often shall my brother sin against me, and I forgive him? As many as seven times?' Our love is as boundless as the love of God, and so Jesus answered, 'I do not say to you seven times, but seventy times seven.'

Therefore the kingdom of heaven may be compared to a king who wished to settle with his servants. When he began the reckoning, one was brought to him who owed him ten thousand talents; and as he could not pay, his lord ordered him to be sold, with his wife and children and all that he had, and payment to be made. So the servant fell on his knees, imploring him, 'Lord, have patience with me and I will pay you everything.' And out of pity for him, the lord of that servant released him and forgave him the debt.

But that same servant, as he went out, came upon one of his fellow servants who owed him a hundred denarii; and seizing him by the throat he said, 'Pay me what you

owe.' So his fellow servant fell down and besought him,
'Have patience with me, and I will pay you.' He refused
and went and put him in prison till he should pay the debt.
When his fellow servants saw what had taken place, they
were greatly distressed, and they went and reported to their
lord all that had taken place. Then his lord summoned him
and said to him, 'You wicked servant! I forgave you all that
debt because you besought me; and should not you have had
mercy on your fellow servant as I had mercy on you?' And
in anger his lord delivered him to the jailers, till he should
pay all his debt.

So also my heavenly Father will do to every one of you,
if you do not forgive your brother from your heart. (Matthew
18:21–35)

Free gift though it is that God forgives our sins, whatever
they may be, there is one prerequisite – that we are sorry
we have grieved his heart of love. There is a common
sentimentality today which forgets the need for penitence.
A Christian minister who was mugged and beaten or who
had his home burgled and vandalised would be asked by the
media, 'Do you forgive your attacker?' And if he answered,
as well he might, 'Of course I do – we must always forgive
those who offend us, and so I won't be pressing charges,' he
would be praised as a man of God who lived by his principles
even when he had suffered greatly. Yet that is not Christian
forgiveness but a weak sentimentality, for no penitence was
shown and the community was still at risk from those who
had escaped punishment.

On the other hand, a recent report told how someone robbed
a church's collection box and left a note, 'Sorry about this, but
my kids had no food.' The wonder of God's love is that He will
accept us even when our penitence is limited and we cannot
perceive the reality of the wrong we have done. There are
moral absolutes and the commandment, Thou shalt not steal,
is one of them. But the failure to pay a debt is a form of theft
since it takes from another that which is their own property.

Yet Jesus commended the lord who 'out of pity' released the servant from his huge debt because he had begged him, 'Lord, have patience with me and I will pay you everything.'

That is far from the moral relativism which has plagued the Church's thinking and attitudes since the early sixties – a new morality only a little removed from the old immorality.

It was in 1963 that John Robinson's book, *Honest to God*, burst on an unsuspecting world, initially serialised in a Sunday newspaper. It was an instant success in a decade which prided itself on its iconoclastic propensities and it rapidly became an unlikely best-seller. Its author, Dr J. A. T. Robinson, had formerly been a Cambridge don, but at the time of the book's publication had been suffragan Bishop of Woolwich in the diocese of Southwark for some four years.

Of his book, Robinson commented at the time that 'it will seem to be radical, and doubtless to many heretical. The one thing of which I am fairly sure is that, in retrospect, it will be seen to have erred in not being radical enough.' Thirty years later, it can be said that for some the latter assessment is certainly true, and within the Church of England it is fair to say that not a few of our theological schools are dominated by teaching which is far more radical than the hesitant heresies chronicled by Robinson in *Honest to God*.

Robinson himself was a scholar of great integrity and honesty. He was not one of those, polemicist rather than scholar, who would come to a radical conclusion and then search for such evidence as might support it, while carefully excluding any invalidating testimony. Later in his career, when he had returned to the academic life to which he was more suited, he published in 1976 one of his finest studies, *Redating the New Testament*, in which he came to the conclusion that the whole of the New Testament was written before AD 70.

One reviewer noted that this overturned the judgments of most New Testament scholars throughout the world, raising 'serious if unfashionable questions'. But Robinson was never concerned to be fashionable, and in *The Priority of John*, published posthumously in 1985, he argued persuasively and controversially that the gospel of John was the first to be written, pointing to a direct authorship by John himself. It did not endear him to his fellow New Testament scholars, but Robinson would never postulate a 'popular' solution if his scholarship led him to a different conclusion. He was a pure and incorruptible radical, and a liberal in the true sense of that much misused word. He was a rare bird in the academic world of his day, of a *genus* which today seems almost extinct.

Robinson did not create the concept of a 'new morality' but rather he examined and distilled thoughts and ideas set out by scholars such as Emil Brunner and Paul Tillich. But he did give it a popular form, and if any one person can lay claim to introducing the new morality to a wider public, it has to be John Robinson.

It is an ethic centred – attractively – on love.

> Love alone, because, as it were, it has a built-in moral compass, enabling it to 'home' intuitively upon the deepest need of the other, can allow itself to be directed completely by the situation. (*Honest to God*, SCM, 1963, p. 115)

Situation ethics is an ethic of 'radical responsiveness' which meets every situation openly and only on its own merits, without any prescriptive laws, without any religious moral code, free for ever to respond to the immediate situation:

> It is prepared to see every moment as a fresh creation from God's hand demanding its own and perhaps wholly unprecedented reponse. (*Honest to God*, p. 115)
> It is a radical 'ethic of the situation', with nothing prescribed – except love. (*Honest to God*, p. 116)

Robinson regards it not as a new morality, but simply as none other than the old, with an emphasis on the commandment to love one another. He compares it to St Augustine's famous dictum, '*Dilige et quod vis fac*', 'Love and do what you please' (*Honest to God*, p. 119), which he suggests correctly translated should read, 'Love and then what you will, do.'

In situation ethics, that we care enough for another is the basis of ethical behaviour rather than the setting of rules and prohibitions. Love, caring, is the criterion for every form of behaviour, 'for *nothing else* makes a thing right or wrong' (*Honest to God*, p.119). Unfortunately for the Christian this ignores the need to see the place which law had in the mission and teaching of Jesus, who came not to abolish the law but to fulfil it: 'For truly, I say to you, till heaven and earth pass away, not an iota, not a dot, will pass from the law till all is accomplished' (Matthew 5:18).

Moreover, in practical terms, to claim that how I love someone is all that matters, that 'nothing else makes a thing right or wrong', is to disregard the reality of the human condition. St Paul, who understood human nature better than we would often give him credit for, expressed it well when he said of himself, I can will what is right, but I cannot do it. For I do not do the good I want, but the evil that I do not want is what I do' (Romans 7:18–19).

The ideal which Robinson describes is persuasive and laudable: but it is an ideal which founders on the rock of human nature. If we could truly say, 'I behave like this towards you because I love you', and say it in full awareness of any hidden motives or desires – that is, if we could see ourselves as only God can see us – then a situation ethic based only on love might work. It might produce a society where each cared for the other, utterly, totally and dispassionately, a society where there was no violence, no exploitation, no abuse.

But life is not like that and we are not like that. If we were, there would have been no need for the cross, no place for redemption, no understanding that God can bring us to Himself and make us what He intends us to be only when we commit ourselves totally to Him. It was a concept which was intended to be a force for good and instead became one of the factors in the terrible decline of society's values which has so damaged the quality and decency of human existence in our western society.

It came at precisely the wrong time. Love was the byword of the sixties generation, yet that was a decade which proved almost totally destructive of common values, from bad architecture constructed from the shoddiest of materials to the abandonment of moral standards in the name of a spurious freedom, in favour of a shoddiness of life from which we still seek to recover.

Jesus was more worldly wise and recognised the reality of human nature. He had been teaching in the Temple when a group of scribes and Pharisees brought a woman before him. She had committed adultery, 'caught in the very act'. What, they ask, does he say should be done to her since the law of Moses commands that she should be stoned?

Of course it is a trick question. We know from the words used by Jewish religious leaders when they brought Jesus before Pilate for sentence that to stone her to death would be against the state law: 'It is not lawful for us to put anyone to death', they were to tell Pilate. But would Jesus insist that they hold to the law of Moses or the law of Rome?

The less international trick to the question is also at the heart of the Church's problem today in dealing with moral matters: to condemn or to condone? Jesus turns the challenge on the woman's accusers: 'Let him who is without sin cast the first stone.' There is a pause as the men consider their own consciences and their own sinfulness, and then each of them, beginning with the eldest, goes away, leaving the woman alone with Jesus.

They have not condemned her, and, so the argument would go today, nor should church leaders condemn sinners but rather follow the example of the Jesus whom they are supposed to serve.

In the story of the woman taken in adultery, God through Moses has set the law and is the judge of all things. And the law is clear: that a woman taken in adultery must be stoned, a punishment which the men are ready and willing to execute.

As 'jury', they have accepted her guilt, for she was 'caught in the very act', and this Jesus does not question – indeed as a jury member, as it were co-opted by the scribes and Pharisees, he shares the recognition of her guilt, saying to her when all have left, 'Go and *sin* no more.' The mistake of those who brought her before Jesus was that they wished to be her executioner as well as the jury which declared the law.

Or put the story in a modern setting, in the troubles of Northern Ireland where even after the cease-fire, Protestant and Catholic (that is, nationalist and republican) paramilitaries were still roaming in armed gangs, punishing those whom they believed to be wrong-doers. There was of course no judge or jury to establish guilt, merely a cruel and arbitrary beating or knee-capping or execution.

And seeing that a crowd had gathered around Jesus, the paramilitaries brought before him a young woman accused of drug-dealing. 'We have caught this woman in the very act of dealing, with crack-cocaine and ecstasy tablets on her. She has admitted that she is the one who supplied the tablet which killed the teenager. She has offended against our code and we say a life for a life. What do you say about her?' This they said to test him, that the ordinary people would turn against him if he failed to join the common desire to stamp out an evil trade. At first he said nothing, and their anger and taunts increased.

Then he stood up and said to the paramilitaries, 'Let him who is without sin, who has never offended against your code of law, fire the first shot.' And one by one they went away, as Jesus' gaze seemed to search into the soul. The first left as he thought of the occasion when he killed for revenge and against orders; the second as the guilt surfaced that while on active service duty she herself had committed adultery, and with the husband of a sister she loved. In the end, only their leader remained and Jesus looked into his eyes.

The man averted his gaze as he thought of the day when, against all orders, he revealed to his wife the details of an action which was about to take place. She told her mother, her mother told a friend, and the friend told another who was a police informer. Soldiers were ready in ambush and he was the only member of the cell to survive the attack. Casting his eyes down, he left quietly.

Jesus said to the woman, 'Has no-one condemned you?' She replied, 'No-one, sir.' Jesus said, 'Neither do I condemn you; go, and do not sin again.'

He did not for a moment condone the woman's drug-dealing, nor did he excuse what she had done by a misplaced liberality which excused her: 'I understand that you needed the money because an acquisitive society and uncaring government has made you homeless and unemployed.' His words, 'Neither do I condemn you', were a refusal to join in a careless and unjust human act of judgment that might have cost her her life. And his comment to her not to sin again was no paternalistic, 'Run along, and be a good girl in future', but a divine injunction to obey the laws of God.

Elsewhere, Jesus gives a clear direction and warning against going a step further and taking the place of God as judge:

'Judge not, that you be not judged. For with the judgement you pronounce you will be judged, and the measure you give will be the measure you get.' (Matthew 7:1)

In other words, if we ourselves take on the role which only God can occupy, then we must expect, not the pure, absolute, perfect and utterly fair judgment which He would perform, but a defective judgment which would inevitably be marred by our own imperfections.

To be morally relative or morally absolute, to be judgmental or compassionate, to condone or to condemn – it is a minefield for human understanding and little wonder if we often take a wrong path. But God has set certain standards which remain; yet at the same time He is Love, all-knowing, all-comprehending Love and He alone is our final judge. We know that it is and will eternally be a fair and just judgment; and we know also that He so loved us that He 'sent his Son to be the expiation for our sins' (1 John 4:10).

That is the good news which is the gospel of Jesus Christ. Without it, the Bible is without significance; and without it, our life has no meaning and no purpose and no hope.

14

End and Beginning

At the end of forty years wandering in the wilderness, Moses stood on Mount Nebo, to the east of Jericho and above the northern tip of the Dead Sea.

And the Lord showed him all the land, Gilead as far as Dan, all Naphtali, the land of Ephraim and Manasseh, all the land of Judah as far as the Western Sea, the Negeb, and the Plain, that is, the Valley of Jericho the city of palm trees, as far as Zoar. And the Lord said to him, 'This is the land of which I swore to Abraham, to Isaac, and to Jacob, "I will give it to your descendants." I have let you see it with your eyes, but you shall not go over there.' So Moses the servant of the Lord died there in the land of Moab. (Deuteronomy 34:1–5)

It was the end of the journey. It was the end of the journey which came from God's call to Moses, full of privations, disappointments, wonders, achievements, all under the leading of the God who first called. It was the end too of the slavery in Egypt and of the wilderness wanderings, and the beginning of a new life in the land to which God had called them and which He had granted them, the people who were the Children of Israel. It was the end too of the journey through this life for Moses, who was called by God to this task, who saw that call through to its end, but did not see its result. But then those who are called of God do not always see the cause, or the entire purpose, or the final fulfilment.

It was not a vast area, the land from Dan to Beersheba out to the Western Sea, and almost within the limit of sight from the heights of Mount Nebo. Dan was about a hundred miles northwards up the Great Rift Valley; the sea, the Mediterranean, some sixty miles to the west; and Beersheba sixty-five miles towards the south-west. It would have been as if we were to stand on a high point of the North Yorkshire Moors with Berwick-on-Tweed and the Scottish border to the north, the Irish Sea to the west and the Peak District hills to the south-west; or on the Chiltern Hills with the Peak District to the north, the Severn Estuary to the west and Winchester in the south-west. Little more than the size of a pin-prick on the vastness of the planet, but where the salvation of all mankind was determined.

For the Israelites it was the end but also the beginning, for the land to which God had led them must be conquered. The northern limit of the land was to mark another end and beginning, though the disciples of Jesus were not to be aware of this until hindsight revealed it. For it was to Dan in the north, and indeed beyond Dan to Caesarea Philippi that Jesus led his followers for a time alone together before his final passion and death, a symbolic withdrawal to the edge of the Promised Land itself for the final preparations.

Caesarea Philippi is a beautiful and peaceful place, beside one of the sources of the Jordan river. I visited it in 1982, at the time when Israel had just invaded the Lebanon, and our bus drove into a car-park empty of all but a military jeep, with four or five soldiers lounging by the food-kiosk. They told us they had just come across the border (some three or four miles away) to have lunch away from the fighting.

Political problems had made it impossible for us to visit the usual site where the baptism of Jesus is commemorated, and so after we had eaten we walked by the stream and into the woods, to hear the baptism story and celebrate the event. Some of our party waded into the shallow Jordan, while others sat on the bank and dipped their feet into the water. I sat a little further back and was suddenly aware of a rustling in the undergrowth behind me. I peered into the gloom and saw a soldier, in full battle-dress and carrying an automatic rifle, creeping round.

I am not by nature apt to panic in such circumstances and I waited to see what would develop. After a few moments, having heard that we were praying rather than plotting, he stood up and came forward. He was an older man for a soldier, perhaps in his mid-forties, and he told us that he had been away from home for four weeks and had been unable to contact his wife and family. Did any of us speak Israeli, and if so, could we telephone his wife when we returned to our hotel to let her know that he was safe and well? Our tour leader, an Anglican priest based in Jerusalem, said he did and took the telephone number.

There was danger in the air throughout our visit to Caesarea Philippi; but it was good to be served a reminder that there was a premonition of danger too when Jesus was there with his disciples. But first he must know if the time was ripe for them to be told plainly what the future held; so he asked them:

'Who do men say the Son of Man is?' And they said, 'Some say John the Baptist, others say Elijah, and others Jeremiah or one of the prophets.' He said to them, 'But who do you say that I am?' (Matthew 16:14–15)

It was a challenge more than a question. They must often have discussed among themselves if he was indeed the Christ, the Messiah who was to come, or if he embodied the promised return of Elijah or of another prophet. Now Simon Peter stepped forward, answering challenge with challenge: 'You are the Christ, the Son of the living God.'

A moment of tension, an expectant silence as the disciples turned towards Jesus to see how he would react. Then perhaps he would look Simon Peter in the eye, stretch out his arms to hold him by the shoulders; and after a moment he answered him, in a quiet but contented voice: "'Blessed are you, Simon

Bar-Jona! For flesh and blood has not revealed this to you but my Father who is in heaven"' (Matthew 16:17).

There was more for Simon: for he was henceforth to be Peter – *petros*, from the Greek *petra*, a rock.

'And on this rock I will build my church, and the powers of earth shall not prevail against it. I will give you the keys of the kingdom of heaven, and whatever you bind on earth shall be bound in heaven, and whatever you loose on earth shall be loosed in heaven.' Then he strictly charged the disciples to tell no one that he was the Christ. (Matthew 16:18–20)

It was an awesome commission. First for Simon Peter himself, who for all his bravado, his undoubted courage, his fearlessness in speaking out, knew only too well that underneath there was weakness. But it is in this that he represents all of us; for it is not on our strength that the Church of God is built, but rather on our weaknesses and failures. St Paul gives a firm reminder of this:

For consider your call, brethren; not many of you were wise according to worldly standards, not many were powerful, not many were of noble birth; but God chose what is foolish in the world to shame the wise, God chose what is weak in the world to shame the strong. God chose what is low and despised in the world, even things that are not, to bring to nothing things that are, so that no human being might boast in the presence of God. He is the source of your life in Christ Jesus, whom God made our wisdom, our righteousness and sanctification and redemption; therefore, as it is written, 'Let him who boasts, boast of the Lord.' (1 Corinthians 1:26–31)

It is an awesome commission too for the Church and for the people who are the Church, the Body of Christ. For it demands that there be no retreat in the face of danger or persecution or difficulty; and that we never despair however dark may seem

the valley in which we dwell. There have been many times in
the Church's history when its state was so parlous that it could
be saved by no human agency. Yet it survives, and emerges
renewed and refreshed – not always of course in such a form
as its members might expect or hope, but ready for God's
purpose. Its truths can be ridiculed, undermined, denied, even
by those who claim to be its faithful servants and scholars.
But even the gates of hell cannot prevail against it.

For we are never alone. There is a constant battle in which
we must join in whatever way God may call us, sometimes
in fulfilment of St Paul's words: 'We are not contending
against flesh and blood, but against the principalities, against
the powers, against the world rulers of this present darkness,
against the spiritual hosts of wickedness in the heavenly places'
(Ephesians 6:12).

Sometimes we may not even be aware of the part we have
played in God's plan and purpose, for we are called not to
success or even to comprehension, only to faithfulness. In
C. S. Lewis's third religious-cum-science fiction novel, *That
Hideous Strength*, there is a giant conspiracy against the
human race which, if it were successful, could destroy all
that is good in humanity. Against the forces of evil, in a centre
of goodness close by the conspiracy's headquarters, a small
group of ill-sorted, ineffective folk are gathered together.

When the forces of evil have been defeated, a member of
the tiny group says, 'I'd be greatly obliged if anyone could
tell me what we *have* done – apart from always feeding the
pigs and raising some very decent vegetables.' He is told by
the Director (who is not Christ, but certainly is a figure or
pattern for him), 'You have done what was required of you.
You have obeyed and waited. It will often happen like that.'
(*That Hideous Strength*, Pan, 1955, pp. 241–2)

Maybe at times we need the reassurance which was granted
to the servant of Elisha the prophet, when the armies of the
king of Syria laid siege to the city of Dothan.

When the servant of the man of God rose early in the

morning and went out, behold, an army with horses and chariots was round about the city. And the servant said, 'Alas, my master! What shall we do?' He said, 'Fear not, for those who are with us are more than those who are with them.' Then Elisha prayed, and said, 'O Lord, I pray thee, open his eyes that he may see.' So the Lord opened the eyes of the young man, and he saw; and behold, the mountain was full of horses and chariots of fire round Elisha. (2 Kings 6:15–17)

But there is more than this in the story of Jesus with his disciples at Caesarea Philippi. Now that they had acknowledged his Messiahship, they must learn something of its true meaning and purpose. It would be not only unexpected but perhaps also unacceptable – as indeed it was to Simon Peter. For it was from the moment of that confession of Peter at Caesarea Philippi, when they accepted Jesus as the Christ who was to come, that he was able to show his disciples that it would be necessary for him to go up to Jerusalem, not to be greeted as Messiah but to suffer at the hands of their religious leaders, to be put to death, and – more extraordinary – to be raised again on the third day after his death. Simon Peter would have none of it:

And Peter took him and began to rebuke him, saying, 'God forbid, Lord! This shall not happen to you.' But he turned and said to Peter, 'Get behind me, Satan! You are a hindrance to me; for you are not on the side of God, but of men.' (Matthew 16:22–3)

So he who was Peter, the Rock, buoyed up by the honour and the responsibility which that title laid upon him, learnt the hardest way possible that what he thought was his strength was in reality weakness. Called by his master 'Satan', 'a hindrance', charged as one who was 'not on the side of God, but of men' – it was more than a blow to pride, and we might imagine the hurt silence to which this fearsome censure would have reduced him. Nowhere and to nobody did Jesus deliver a stronger rebuke than to the one who was the Rock on which the Church would be built.

But it is not only their master who must suffer in the fulfilment of God's call. With Peter standing by, shocked and silent, Jesus then spoke to all the disciples:

> 'If any man would come after me, let him deny himself and take up his cross and follow me. For whoever would save his life will lose it, and whoever loses his life for my sake will find it. For what will it profit a man if he gains the whole world and forfeits his life?' (Matthew 16:24–6)

Not far from the river in Caesarea Philippi is a rock face into which the Greeks and Romans carved niches for statues of their gods. From it the mountains climb quickly becoming what we know today as the Golan Heights. It feels to the visitor to be the end of the road, a cul-de-sac from which the only exit is a return to the land of biblical Israel. Now that the disciples had acknowledged that he was the Christ who was to come, Jesus could set out on the final journey which was to end on the cross at Calvary.

15

Transfiguration

Danger was never far away from Jesus in his ministry and on his preaching journeys. In the earliest days after his temptations in the wilderness, he visited his home town of Nazareth, the local boy made good, known to be making a name for himself as a preacher and teacher throughout Galilee. They were proud of him and of the honour his growing fame brought to their city. Of course he was invited to 'say a few words' at the Sabbath service in the synagogue.

And he stood up to read; and there was given to him the book of the prophet Isaiah. He opened the book and found the place where it was written:

'The Spirit of the Lord is upon me, because he has anointed me to preach good news to the poor. He has sent me to proclaim release to the captives and recovering of sight to the blind, to set at liberty those who are oppressed, to proclaim the acceptable year of the Lord.'

And he closed the book, and gave it back to the attendant and sat down; and the eyes of all in the synagogue were fixed upon him. And he began to say to them, 'Today this scripture has been fulfilled in your sight.' (Luke 4:17–21)

It was a tense moment and they fixed their eyes on him with

expectation and pride. At first his hearers were happy, and they
murmured with appreciation at his gracious words.

> And they said, 'Is not this Joseph's son?' And he said
> to them, 'Doubtless you will quote to me this proverb,
> "Physician, heal yourself; what we have heard you do in
> Capernaum, do here also in your own country."' And he
> said, 'Truly, I say to you, no prophet is acceptable in his
> own country.' (Luke 4:22–3)

It was beginning to go awry, to move in a wrong direction.
They listened with dismay and growing offence as he told
of the great famine in the days of Elijah and the many
widows with nothing to eat. But Elijah was sent to none,
but instead ministered to the Sidonian widow, Zarephath.
And he told of the lepers in the days of Elisha; but only the
Syrian Naaman was cleansed by God through the prophet.
It was as if he was saying to them, 'Yes, I can give you my
Father's message; but you will not listen, any more than the
people of Israel listened to the message of the prophets of
God before me.'

> When they heard this, all in the synagogue were filled with
> wrath. And they rose up and put him out of the city, and led
> him to the brow of a hill on which their city was built, that
> they might throw him down headlong. But passing through
> the midst of them he went away. (Luke 4:28–30)

This time he escaped the crowd's wrath, perhaps somehow
carried along in a vast throng, too many to notice one man
edging his way out of it; or maybe, spirited away by his friends
and supporters.

Not far from Nazareth are the ruins of Belvoir Castle, a
Crusader fort built on the escarpment overlooking the Jordan
Valley. From one point in the gardens, one can see the sharp
brow of the hill from which they sought to cast him and, behind

it, the cone-shaped Mount Tabor. A careful photographer with a long lens can superimpose one upon the other, as if they are close. For me, it was a reminder of death and glory which is so much a part of the story of Jesus: the danger of death from the very earliest days of the ministry, and the glory which was seen on Mount Tabor, the traditional site for the Transfiguration of Jesus.

It was only six days after the events at Caesarea Philippi that Jesus took the inner circle of his apostles, Peter, James and John, the brother of James, to a 'high mountain apart'. 'And he was transfigured before them, and his face shone like the sun, and his garments became white as light. And behold, there appeared to them Moses and Elijah, talking with him' (Matthew 17:2–3).

There was in the Jewish understanding a connection between mountains and a special presence of God. When Moses received the Ten Commandments from God, it was on the top of a mountain, Mount Sinai, that the transaction was completed.

'Then Moses went up on the mountain, and the cloud covered the mountain. The glory of the Lord settled on Mount Sinai, and the cloud covered it six days; and on the seventh day he called to Moses out of the midst of the cloud' (Exodus 24:15–16).

God's presence was often cloaked by a cloud. When he led the children of Israel from Egypt to the Promised Land, they were guided by a pillar of cloud by day and a pillar of fire by night. 'And the Lord went before them by day in a pillar of cloud to lead them along the way, and by night in a pillar of fire to give them light, that they might travel by day and by night' (Exodus 13:21).

The prophet Isaiah described a land and a people of Israel cleansed and redeemed by God. 'Then the Lord will create over the whole site of Mount Zion and over her assemblies a cloud by day, and smoke and the shining of a flaming fire by night; for over all the glory there will be a canopy and a pavilion' (Isaiah 4:5).

So too when the earthly ministry of Jesus had ended, he needed to show his followers that, yes, he had indeed risen from the dead and was with them till the end of time; but that they would see him no more in this life. So he 'ascended' to the Father: he went up the mountain and a cloud received him from their sight. Not so much a miraculous happening but simply a visual aid, so that they would comprehend, from their own tradition, that he had returned to the Father.

When Jesus took Peter, James and John apart up Mount Tabor (if indeed this was the mount of the transfiguration story), they would understand, by instinct if not by conscious thought, that he was bringing them closer to the Father's presence. And when Jesus was transfigured, so that his face 'shone like the sun', they could not but have been reminded of Moses on Mount Sinai.

> When Moses came down from Mount Sinai, with the two tables of the testimony in his hand, Moses did not know that the skin of his face shone because he had been talking with God. And when Aaron and all the people of Israel saw Moses, behold the skin of his face shone, and they were afraid to come near him. (Exodus 34:29–30)

It is an awesome moment, intensified when they are suddenly aware that Jesus is not alone, but talking with two others whom they identify as Moses and Elijah. As usual Peter in his enthusiasm gets it wrong:

> And Peter said to Jesus, 'Lord, it is well that we are here; if you wish, I will make three booths here, one for you and one for Moses and one for Elijah.' (Matthew 17:4)

But Peter and his fellows were not with Jesus to 'do', but to 'be'. It was one of those moments, rare even in a lifetime of faith, when a corner of the veil is lifted to display a sudden brief glimpse of the glory of the living God.

I have known such moments. Sometimes it has been in

music: the first time I heard Bach's *Mass in B minor*, when to listen to the *Crucifixus* and *Et Resurrexit* was to hear the voices of angels lamenting the death and glorying in the life of the Son of God, and to know surely a music touched by the finger of God. Music too at the funeral of Canon Gareth Bennett, driven to take his own life by the pressures around him: as the choir in the dark and candle-lit chapel at New College, Oxford, sang the Burial Sentences,

> Thou knowest, Lord, the secrets of our hearts:
> shut not thy merciful ears to our prayer.
> But spare us, Lord most holy,
> O God most mighty, O holy and most merciful Saviour,
> Thou most worthy judge eternal,
> suffer us not at our last hour
> for any pains of death to fall from thee.

The pain at the tragic and unnecessary death of a friend was not eased; but in a moment I knew – knew and felt – the love of a God who understood the secrets of the heart, and who wiped away the sin which destroys that which it is not in man's gift to destroy.

One Ash Wednesday, I preached in the chapel of St Stephen's House, an Oxford seminary, and at the communion, the choir sang the hauntingly beautiful *Miserere*, by Allegri.

> Have mercy upon me, O God, after thy great goodness:
> according to the multitude of thy mercies do away mine
>   offences
> Wash me throughly from my wickedness:
> and cleanse me from my sin.
>
> (Psalm 51, Book of Common Prayer)

Originally sung only in the Sistine Chapel (until Mozart committed it to memory and transcribed it), one traveller who heard it in Rome described it as 'groans to rend the heart'.

There is truly the deep sadness brought by a recognition of one's sinfulness; but then soaring treble voices come as a glorious reminder of the salvation wrought by Christ on the cross. It was the opening of a gate into heaven.

I have known such moments too in the beauty of creation: in the wind and silence of the North Yorkshire Moors, as the ridges stretch, line upon line, to the horizon and beyond sight; in the gentle loveliness of the Sussex downs, in the majesty of the Alps and the Rockies, speechless at their splendour. In the beauty of human creation when it has been touched by God; at a first teenage sight of York Minster, or the interior of St David's Cathedral in Wales; in a country church whose very stones have been saturated by centuries of prayer; holding an ancient chalice, battered and worn, but with a date like 1547 or 1662 which echoes the dangers which faith brought to the faithful in its use.

Moments too in the serenity of human companionship: the first sight of a baby son's smile and the moment when, worried that I could not cope with the pain and joy of parenthood, I heard the words, as clearly as if they had been from a voice in the same room. 'Do not you think I will look after him?' Or the moments of quiet tranquillity in marriage with the certain assurance that one loves and is loved 'for naught except for love's sake only' (Elizabeth Barrett Browning, *Sonnets from the Portuguese XIV*). With the best of friends too, moments in their presence when one knows that the friendship is cemented by a loyalty which is for ever and which can bear all.

Such rare and precious moments never diminish but only deepen the knowledge that God is with us always, that, in the Psalmist's words,

Such knowledge is too wonderful and excellent for me:
    I cannot attain unto it.
Whither shall I go then from thy Spirit:
    or whither shall I go then from thy presence?
If I climb up into heaven, thou art there:
    if I go down to hell, thou art there also.
                    (Psalm 139:5–7 Book of Common Prayer)

On the mount of transfiguration, Peter's human and inadequate response was ignored as the experience, already deep and beyond understanding, was further enhanced.

He (Peter) was still speaking, when lo, a bright cloud overshadowed them, and a voice from the cloud said, 'This is my beloved Son, in whom I am well pleased: listen to him.' When the disciples heard this, they were filled with awe. But Jesus came and touched them, saying, 'Rise, and have no fear.' And when they lifted up their eyes, they saw no-one but Jesus only. (Matthew 17:5–8)

The experience was over and they must come down from the mountain – figuratively as well as literally. For when they returned to the rest of their company, they found a crowd gathered and a man angry and bitter that the other disciples had been unable to cure his epileptic son. From the opening of heaven's doors to the closing of men's minds – it was too much, and Jesus responded, angrily, '"O faithless and perverse generation, how long am I to be with you? How long am I to bear with you? Bring him to me"' (Matthew 17:17).

And with a word and a touch, Jesus cured the boy instantly.

The disciples' faith was not enough; yet, they were told, if they had 'faith as a grain of mustard seed' they could remove mountains. Nevertheless they must still be prepared and be ready for what was to come.

As they were gathering in Galilee, Jesus said to them, 'The Son of man is to be delivered into the hands of men, and they will kill him, and he will be raised on the third day.' And they were greatly distressed. (Matthew 17:22–3)

16

Death and Life

Jesus made his last visit to Jerusalem before the Passover
festival at which he was crucified during the previous winter.
It was the December festival of Dedication, commemorated
today by Jewish people as *Hanukkah* and commemorating the
purification of the Temple after its defilement in 170 BC by
Antiochus Epiphanes. Jesus offended the religious leaders by
claiming, 'I and the Father are one.' At first they took up
stones to kill him and when later he repeated the claim, with
the words, 'The Father is in me and I am in the Father,' they
tried unsuccessfully to arrest him (John 10:22–39; and see also
chapter 7).

In the four months between Dedication and Passover, Jesus
avoided the limelight and kept away from the city of Jerusalem,
spending time across the Jordan at 'the place where John first
baptised' (John 10:40). But personal love and loyalty was to
bring him again into danger, when a close friend, Lazarus of
Bethany, the brother of his Martha and Mary, became unwell.
(For a deeper reflection on Mary, the brother of Lazarus, see
chapter 17.)

The sisters sent word to Jesus that his friend was seriously
ill. His response was unexpected. 'This illness,' he declared,
'is not unto death; it is for the glory of God.' And instead of
going immediately to Bethany, a village about three miles to
the west of Jerusalem, beyond the Mount of Olives and on
the road to Jericho, he stayed a further two days beyond the

Jordan. The disciples must have assumed that Lazarus's illness was less serious than his sisters had suggested.

After two days, he told the disciples that they would now return to Judea. It was dangerous for them, and the disciples questioned the decision, reminding him that on his last visit the religious authorities had tried to stone him. (It is well for modern readers to remind themselves that when St John speaks of 'the Jews' doing this or that to Jesus, it is short for 'the Jewish religious authorities' and we might say 'the Church' when we mean its leadership. The modern tendency to suggest that St John's Gospel is anti-Semitic is mistaken and damaging.)

Jesus then revealed to his followers the more pressing reason why they must set out towards the dangers of Jerusalem:

> 'Our friend Lazarus has fallen asleep, but I go to wake him out of sleep.' The disciples said to him, 'Lord, if he has fallen asleep, he will recover.' Now Jesus had spoken of his death, but they thought he meant taking rest in sleep. Then Jesus told them plainly, 'Lazarus is dead; but for your sake I am glad I was not there, so that you may believe. But let us go to him.' (John 11:11–15)

The disciples were clearly uneasy with his decision and reluctant to join him on the journey, but Thomas persuaded them: 'Let us also go, that we may die with him.' When they arrived at Bethany, they found that Lazarus was dead and had already been in the tomb for four days. Martha and Mary were not alone, for friends, as well probably as professional mourners from Jerusalem, had arrived to console them at their brother's death.

The different reactions of the two sisters at Jesus' delayed arrival will be familiar to anyone accustomed to ministry to the bereaved. For bereavement often brings with it anger: anger against doctors, nurses, friends or relations who may be thought to have contributed to the death; anger against other members of the family for whom death may need to be faced in another way to one's own way; and of course anger against God which often cannot dare to be expressed but finds its outlet if the hapless minister quite inadvertently makes a mistake of some kind to upset the mourners.

From Martha and Mary there is resentment that Jesus has taken so long to respond. 'Did he not get the message?' Martha might have asked Peter or Thomas. 'Then why didn't he come at once? I thought he really cared about Lazarus – and about us. Mary is so upset and angry – I don't think she'll speak to him. She feels really let down.'

But Martha was ready to meet him, to give him the benefit of the doubt. He is so good a friend, there must be a very good reason why he didn't set out at once. When they met, outside the village, Martha said to him, quietly with sadness, '"Lord, if you had been here, my brother would not have died. And even now I know that whatever you ask from God, God will give you.' Jesus said to her, "Your brother will rise again"' (John 11:21–23).

We make ritual comments at a bereavement, no less kind or comforting because they are what we feel we must say. 'At least he didn't suffer.' 'She's at peace now after so much pain.' And so on. When Jesus said, 'Your brother will rise again', Martha took it in those terms, a phrase one says on such occasions and one with which others had already tried to comfort her when really they knew that nothing – save their very presence, the fact that they cared enough to be there – could dull the pain which the sisters felt.

The ritual comment was almost expected. What followed could not have been more unexpected. For Jesus then added words which, now read as a body is carried into church for the Funeral Service, have since brought comfort to many a broken heart:

'I am the resurrection and the life; he who believes in me, though he die, yet shall he live, and whoever lives and believes in me shall never die. Do you believe *this*?' (John 11:25–6)

Did she believe this? Indeed she did, and more; and as her heart leapt for joy and her spirits were restored, she confessed her faith in him, as Peter had done at Caesarea Philippi. 'Yes, Lord; I believe that you are the Christ, the Son of God, he who is coming into the world.' Perhaps she had wanted to declare it before but had until now lacked the courage or the certainty. Now it poured out: oh yes, she believed, believed he really was the Messiah who was to come – the Christ, the Son of God, the one of whose coming the prophets had foretold.

Then Martha returned to the house and told her sister, Mary, 'The Teacher is here and wants to see you. Come along now, do go to him, he's asking for you.' Now Mary quickly arose and went out to the place outside the village where Jesus had talked with Martha. Yes, she would see him, and she'd give him a piece of her mind. He'd let them down and she wasn't afraid of him whoever he thought he was. Sensing a confrontation, those mourners in the house with them followed Mary. If there was to be an argument, they would be at her side. This Jesus had obviously got a little above himself. Well, he'd shown he had feet of clay and now they could have the satisfaction of seeing him taken down a peg or two.

When Mary came to Jesus, she could not meet his eye, but fell at his feet. 'Lord, if you had been here, my brother would not have died.' No quiet rebuke this time, and no softening with Martha's gentle words which followed; and Jesus accepts her anger without response.

When Jesus saw her weeping, and the Jews who came with her also weeping, he was deeply moved in spirit and troubled; and he said, 'Where have you laid him?' They said to him, 'Lord, come and see.' Jesus wept. (John 11:33–5)

To weep in the presence of the death of a loved one is not to lack faith; any more than to weep when a son or daughter is seen off at an airport to take up work at the other side of the world is to doubt they will ever return. But in death there is a separation of time, even if there is a certainty of eternal togetherness. We need tears. The English stiff upper lip is no virtue, but an emotional thrombosis which can damage our own health and our relationships with those around us.

So Jesus wept at the death of his friend and took up the emotions of those standing by. Some said, 'Look at those tears; see how he really loved him.' But others, stirring up the resentment against him, asked, 'Could not he who opened the eyes of the blind man have kept this man from dying?' Jesus ignored them, and came eventually to the tomb, a cave over which lay a heavy stone. 'Take away the stone,' he ordered. Martha was horrified: yes, of course he was upset, but it was too much to demand to see the body.

She objected and pointed out a very practical problem. 'Lord, by this time there will be a stink. Have you forgotten? He's been in there for four days.'

Jesus said to her, 'Did I not tell you that if you would believe you would see the glory of God?' So they took away the stone. And Jesus lifted up his eyes and said, 'Father, I thank thee that thou hast heard me. I knew that thou hearest me always, but I have said this on account of the people standing by, that they may believe that thou didst send me.' When he had said this, he cried with a loud voice, 'Lazarus, come out.' The dead man came out, his hands and feet bound with bandages, and his face wrapped with a cloth. Jesus said to them, 'Unbind him, and let him go.' (John 11:40–44)

What exactly happened? We can never know entirely. The significance of the fact of his having been dead for four days (a corpse would be buried on the day of death because of the quick onset of putrefaction in a hot country) was that the Jewish understanding was of the soul leaving the body after only two days. In other words, Lazarus was truly dead. On the other hand, the recent experience of Mrs Daphne Brown indicates that mistakes can be made, even in our more scientific age.

Mrs Brown was pronounced dead by her local doctor, but in the mortuary the undertaker noticed a faint pulse, then a sign of breathing, and later heard two snores. The 'dead' woman was alive. Did this happen in the case of Lazarus? Not according to Scripture, though that records the interpretation of the event and is not a medical report. While still in the land beyond Jordan, Jesus spoke to the disciples of the death of Lazarus, but this was merely to tell them of the report he had been given of his friend's condition. At no point does Jesus declare that he has raised a dead man.

But that would mean deliberate deception on the part of Jesus if he knew that Lazarus was not in fact dead yet he allowed others to believe he had raised him from the dead. This would be unthinkable: a sin by the divine Son of God, the sinless one. So it must be that Lazarus was indeed dead, and that the four days in which he lay in the tomb was a true indication that, in Jewish understanding of that time, the soul had left the body.

But it was not a resurrection to eternal life, the kind of resurrection which Jesus himself was to undergo soon after this event. To emphasise this, the evangelist, John, records that 'the dead man came out, *his hands and feet bound with bandages, and his face wrapped with a cloth*. Jesus said to them, "Unbind him, and let him go"' (John 11:44).

By contrast, when they heard Mary Magdalene's news that the body of Jesus was no longer in the tomb, Simon Peter and John rushed there to find 'the linen cloths lying, and the napkin, which had been on his head, not lying with the linen cloths, but rolled up in a place by itself' (John 20:6).

This careful description is no accident, but there to provide a deliberate contrast with the story of Lazarus coming out of his tomb.

There were crowds around the tomb who witnessed Lazarus's return – the family, the disciples who had come with Jesus from beyond Jordan, villagers there to share the grief of the two sisters, as well as visitors from Jerusalem, some of them professional mourners. Their reactions were varied, as varied exactly as one would expect.

There were those, supporters and admirers, maybe also some

who until then were unsure of Jesus, who 'believed in him'.
Perhaps they had consoled Martha and Mary during Lazarus's
illness, anxiously watching him as his life expired. They had
seen him dead, helped to prepare the body for burial, and knew
from their own eyes or from the reports of those whom they
trusted that Lazarus had indeed died. Others were less sure: it
must have been a trick, no-one comes back from the dead.
There had been plenty of charlatans posing as prophets – Jesus
was just another. Others again might reject the description of
charlatan but question whether he was really dead.

> But some of them went to the Pharisees and told them
> what Jesus had done. So the chief priests and the Pharisees
> gathered the council, and said, 'What are we to do? For
> this man performs many signs. If we let him go on thus,
> every one will believe in him, and the Romans will come
> and destroy both our holy place and our nation.' (John
> 11:46–8)

It is a dilemma which politicians often face. In a recent
well-publicised case, the British Government sought to deport
a Middle East dissident to an island in the Caribbean. He
was not in any sense a danger either to national security
or to the public, and his primary activity was supplying
anti-government literature and pamphlets to his home country.
But not to deport him might endanger very valuable defence
contracts with the Middle East state. The loss of financial and
economic profit was more important than the avoidance of
injustice.

For the chief priests, Jesus posed a threat to their nation
and, perhaps of more concern, to the religious establishment
and their own position within it. It was a delicate balance
both for Rome and for the council. Emperor worship was
the official religion of the Roman Empire, but the authorities
were sufficiently tolerant to allow these strange Jews, who
believed in one god rather than the panoply of pagan deities
with which they were familiar, to continue in their local ways.

And it kept the peace, where otherwise there could have been conflict and rioting.

But it did compromise the chief priests and council. They would have to tolerate pagan religious activities and idols in the Holy City of Jerusalem. The Roman coinage carried an image of a ruler who was thought to be divine, and for ordinary commerce they must use that currency, except within the precincts of the temple, where animals were bought and sold for sacrifice. Before a transaction took place, Roman coins must be exchanged for temple currency, at a rate which brought much profit to the money-changers.

Caiaphas, who was high priest for that year, was a pragmatist. But there is much evidence in history (as well as in our own time) that as soon as religious leaders are compromised by their accommodation to secular pressures, they are on a slippery slope. The severe warning and injunction which St Paul gave to the Christians in Rome is no less valid today: 'Do not be conformed to this world but be transformed by the renewal of your mind, that you may prove what is the will of God, what is good and acceptable and perfect' (Romans 12:2).

The solution which Caiaphas offered was practical and final: they must get rid of Jesus. He addressed the gathered council: '"You know nothing at all; you do not understand that it is expedient that one man should die for the people, and that the whole nation should not perish"' (John 11:49–50).

St John sees beyond these words to a prophecy which was soon to be fulfilled. 'He did not say this of his own accord, but being high priest for that year he prophesied that Jesus should die for the nation, and not for the nation only, but to gather into one the children of God who are scattered abroad' (John 11:51–2).

So the die is cast and the end is near. Until this point, Jesus has been in charge. He has girded himself and walked where he would. Soon now, others will gird him in clothes he does not choose and then take even these from him. He will walk only where others lead him, he will stretch out his hands and cruel nails will wound the body of the One who healed others.

Jesus therefore no longer went about openly among the Jews, but went from there to the country near the wilderness, to a town called Ephraim; and there he stayed until the Passover. (John 11:54)

17

Bouquets and Brickbats

When I was a small boy before and during the Second World War we lived in Bury, a small cotton town some eight miles north of Manchester. In those days of poor transport, it was an adventure to have a day out in Rochdale or Bolton, each five miles away to the east and west of Bury. To go into Manchester on the ancient electric railway was a rare excitement. Oldham, a little to the south of Rochdale but with no direct road, was a foreign land. It is easy for us today, with our cars and motorways, fast rail transport (at least on the East Coast Line), not to mention the possiblity of flight, to forget that fifty years ago, let alone two thousand years ago, travel was very limited and communication in general primitive and rudimentary.

Ephraim was a town about ten miles to the north of Jerusalem. When Jesus withdrew there with his disciples after the raising of Lazarus it was sufficiently far from the city to be comparatively safe from the attentions of his enemies. But he must be at the Passover festival, and six days before it, he returned to Bethany, probably staying with Lazarus and his sisters.

(St Mark suggests that he was staying 'in the house of Simon the leper' (Mark 14:3) and places the anointing on the Wednesday of Holy Week. But John's is the eye-witness account, and Mark may have confused this story with the anointing on a earlier occasion in the house of Simon the Pharisee (Luke 7:36–50). Or this present meal could have taken place in a neighbour's house in Bethany, the house of Simon the leper. It is not important, and the sort of natural mistake which arises when a story is told second-hand.)

As the little group of disciples made their way on foot from Ephraim, they would probably have avoided the main routes and certainly would not have passed through Jerusalem. Perhaps they passed along the top of the hills surrounding the city and on its eastern edge – Mount Scopus, the Mount of Olives and then down into Bethany.

> There they made him a supper; Martha served, and Lazarus was one of those at table with him. Mary took a pound of costly ointment of pure nard and anointed the feet of Jesus and wiped his feet with her hair; and the house was filled with the fragrance of the ointment. (John 12:2–3)

It was not the first time that Mary had showed her care for him in such a manner. Earlier in the ministry, Jesus had been invited to dinner by a rich Pharisee. It was by no means an invitation between equals, and we can imagine the Pharisee telling his friends, 'Now, you must all come to dinner. We've invited this fellow from Nazareth – a carpenter of all things, behaving like a prophet of God.' 'Oh, what fun! We'll be there.' Jesus was not one to be patronised, and the dinner did not go as planned. The Pharisee, Simon by name, was to meet the unexpected.

> And behold, a woman who was a sinner, when she learned that he was sitting at table in the Pharisee's house, brought an alabaster box of ointment, and standing behind him at his feet, weeping, she began to wet his feet with her tears, and wiped them with the hair of her head, and kissed his feet, and anointed them with the ointment. Now when the Pharisee who had invited him saw it, he said to himself, 'If this man were a prophet, he would have known who and what sort of woman this is who was touching him, for she is a sinner.' (Luke 7:37–9)

There is a fashion today, particularly among American feminist theologians, to reject the identification of the woman who was 'a sinner' (by which almost certainly is meant a prostitute) with Mary Magdalene, and to regard it as a patriarchal and misogynist attack on the virtue of one whom they describe as the first of the apostles. This is an unacceptable sanitisation of one of the loveliest stories in the New Testament. It is far more likely that the evangelists would, in recording the stories, prefer to spare Mary further embarrassment by dwelling on her past, choosing as an act of courtesy and good-will simply to relate the event without naming the main player. It is a mark of the love of God and of the nature of the good news of the gospel that the first witness of the resurrection should be a prostitute whose sins had been forgiven.

When she had completed the act of anointing, Jesus spoke to Simon, aware that he had watched in disapproval as Jesus allowed such a woman to touch his feet. 'Simon,' he said, 'I have something to say to you.'

Perhaps there was an amused smile on Simon's lips, eyebrows raised towards his fellows at the table. 'Yes?' he replied. 'What is it?' A slight pause. 'Teacher?' His friends sniggered. What fun this was! All at this peasant's expense!

> 'A certain creditor had two debtors; one owed five hundred denarii, and the other fifty. When they could not pay, he forgave them both. Now which of them will love him more?' (Luke 7:41–2)

Oh, one of his famous stories – or is it a new game? More sniggers around the table.

> Simon answered, 'The one, I suppose, to whom he forgave more.' And he answered, 'You have judged rightly.' Then turning toward the woman he said to Simon, 'Do you see this woman? I entered your house, you gave me no water for my feet, but she has wet my feet with her tears and wiped

them with her hair. You gave me no kiss, but from the time I came in she has not ceased to kiss my feet. You did not anoint my head with oil, but she has anointed my feet with ointment.' (Luke 7:44–6)

Just as a bishop today is not accustomed to being rebuked by a mere curate, or a prince by a parson, far down the hierarchical pecking-order and altogether a lesser being, so Simon the Pharisee would not relish a reprimand from a carpenter/prophet from Nazareth. The superior smile which had flickered constantly on Simon's lips from the moment Jesus had entered his house was now gone. But there was more to come as Jesus went on, in a firm, strong voice which reverberated around the table, the other guests now silent.

Therefore I tell you, her sins, which are many, are forgiven, for she loved much; he who is forgiven little, loves little.' And he said to her, 'Your sins are forgiven.' Then those who were at table with him began to say among themselves, 'Who is this, who even forgives sins?' And he said to the woman, 'Your faith has saved you; go in peace.' (Luke 7:47–50)

It was a new beginning for Mary; and from that moment Jesus has no more devoted a follower. It is to cause problems for Mary. A little later in Luke's account, Mary had returned home to join her sister Martha.

Now as they went on their way, he entered a village; and a woman named Martha received him into her house. And she had a sister called Mary, who sat at the Lord's feet and listened to his teaching. And Martha was distracted with much serving; and she went to him and said, 'Lord, do you not care that my sister has left me to serve alone? Tell her to help me.' But the Lord answered her, 'Martha, Martha, you are anxious about many things; one thing is needful. Mary has chosen the good portion, which shall not be taken away from her.' (Luke 10:38–42)

So too with the anointing in the house of Simon of Bethany. This time it was Judas Iscariot who complained, Judas who was also the treasurer for the little group of disciples and conscious of the shortages and privations which they had to face in their journeyings, and of the needs of the poor who were always around them, seeking help. The 'waste' of the precious ointment rankled with Judas, and he demanded why it could not have been sold and the money given to the poor.

In an insight more into the character of John himself than that of Judas, the evangelist comments, 'This he said, not that he cared for the poor but because he was a thief, and as he had the money box he used to take what was put into it' (John 12:6).

It is with the benefit of the kind of hindsight which says, when a colleague has fallen from grace, 'Of course I always knew he was a bad 'un, right from the very first time I met him. You could see it in his eyes. I didn't like to say anything at the time.'

Judas's economy, wise and sensible though it may have been, was immediately rebuked by Jesus: '"Let her alone, let her keep it for the day of my burial. The poor you always have with you, but you do not always have me"' (John 12:7–8).

The tension, the premonition of danger about what was to come, soon now, was never far away.

When the great crowd of the Jews learned that he was there, they came, not only on account of Jesus but also to see Lazarus, whom he had raised from the dead. So the chief priests planned to put Lazarus also to death, because on account of him many of the Jews were going away and believing in Jesus. (John 12:9–11)

The Passover festival drew near, and the city of Jerusalem began to fill with pilgrims and worshippers. It was time for the last act to begin and, for it, Jesus had made careful preparations, preparations he had not shared even with his closest followers. One, he knew, would betray him, and nothing must be allowed to go wrong. This was the Passover, and he was the true Passover Lamb of God, the 'one, true, pure, immortal sacrifice', (from the hymn 'And now, O Father, mindful of the love', W. Bright), whose death would supersede all the sacrifices of the Temple worship.

The first preparation was a careful arrangement made secretly with an unknown and unnamed supporter in the village of Bethphage set on the far side from Jerusalem of the Mount of Olives, near to the village of Bethany. There was a messianic prophecy in the book of Zechariah which declared that the 'king' would come into Jerusalem on a donkey.

> Rejoice greatly, O daughter of Zion!
>   Shout aloud, O daughter of Jerusalem!
> Lo, your king comes to you;
>   triumphant and victorious is he,
> humble and riding on an ass,
>   on a colt the foal of an ass. (Zechariah 9:9)

In order to ride into Jerusalem in deliberate fulfilment of this prophecy, Jesus had arranged that his follower in Bethphage, living on the very edge of the village on the road between Bethany and Bethphage, would on a certain day sit by his house and wait. He would have an ass tethered by him and sometime early in the day, two men would approach and take the ass. He was to challenge them, and if they gave the correct password, they were to be allowed to take the animal.

So, on the morning of the day we call Palm Sunday, two disciples were given instructions privately by Jesus:

'Go into the village opposite you, and immediately as you enter it you will find a colt tied, on which no one has ever sat; untie it and bring it. If anyone says to you, "Why are you doing this?"' say, "The Lord has need of it and will send it back here immediately."' And they went away, and found a colt tied at the door out in the open street; and they untied it. (Mark 11:2–4)

They did as instructed and found it exactly as he had told them. When the owner of the ass challenged them, they gave the password and were allowed to take the animal.

> And they brought the colt to Jesus, and threw their garments on it; and he sat upon it. And many spread their garments on the road, and others spread leafy branches which they had cut from the fields. And those who went before and those who followed cried out, 'Hosanna! Blessed is he who comes in the name of the Lord! Blessed is the kingdom of our father David that is coming! Hosanna in the highest!' (Mark 11:7–10)

It was a triumphant entry into the city of Jerusalem and a dramatic one, the deliberate fulfilling of an ancient prophecy in a manner whose meaning was unmistakable to those who witnessed it. It was a declaration by Jesus, 'Yes, I am indeed the Messiah, the one who is to come.' It was a declaration of his kingship, but not a kingship with the trappings of secular power. For this king came 'humble and riding upon an ass'.

The common understanding of the Messiah was that he would be a king, but a ruler under the authority of God who would be the true King of Israel. First he must drive out the hated occupying army of the Romans who had polluted the holiness of the sacred city of Zion not only by their presence but most of all by their pagan and depraved religion.

But the Messiah who was to come would raise an army from the people which would be victorious over the interlopers. In riding into the city at the festival, as Zechariah had foretold, Jesus had only to raise a finger on that day and the people would follow him into battle. The tense anticipation could not have been greater, and the news of his action would have spread like wildfire around the crowded city. Their leaders were horrified at such a turn of events and at the support given to him by the ordinary people. 'The Pharisees then said one to another, "You see that you can do nothing; look, the world has gone after him"' (John 12:19).

It had indeed, at any rate in one sense. There were Greeks at the feast, there to worship, pagans with Jews. It may be that they were converts to the Jewish faith; but to the more orthodox Jews this would be a contradiction, since to be a true Jew one must be Jewish by ancestry as well as by faith. Nevertheless the Greeks came to keep the Passover festival, perhaps finding the purity of the Jewish religion attractive when set against the paganism into which they had been born. They had heard of this prophet from Galilee and came to Philip, perhaps – by reason of his name – believing him to be Greek too. They said to him,

> 'Sir, we wish to see Jesus.' Philip went and told Andrew; Andrew went with Philip and they told Jesus. And Jesus answered them, 'The hour has come for the Son of man to be glorified.' (John 12:21–3)

The Good News which Jesus brought was for all, rich and poor, Jew and Gentile, for those who were slaves and for those who were free. But it was a call to service as well as a call to glory. While the disciples were on their way with Jesus to the festival, puzzled by his constant emphasis on the suffering he must undergo and themselves not a little fearful for their own safety, two of the twelve displayed the poverty of their understanding.

> And James and John, the sons of Zebedee, came forward to him, and said to him, 'Teacher, we want you to do for us whatever we ask of you.' And he said to them, 'What do you want me to do for you?' And they said to him, 'Grant us to sit, one at your right hand and one at your left, in your glory.' But Jesus said to them, 'You do not know what you are asking. Are you able to drink the cup that I drink, or to be baptised with the baptism that I am baptised with?' And they said to him, 'We are able.' (Mark 10:35–9)

'We are able' is a text which has a special memory for me. At the age of seventeen, unattached to a church but certainly not unbelieving, I joined my father at Evensong at St Paul's Bury. My purpose was romantic rather than religious. A group of girls from my school attended and it seemed a way I might get to know them better. (It did not work.) But the visiting preacher that evening was a former vicar, Canon Burnell, and a formidable preacher of his day. His text, delivered in a deep baritone, was 'We are able.' I cannot describe it as a conversion experience: but I do remember it and I was soon confirmed and a regular worshipper.

I can recall nothing else of the sermon. But he might well have spoken of service as its own reward, with glory not to be sought.

And when the ten heard it, they began to be indignant at James and John. And Jesus called them and said to them, 'You know that those who are supposed to rule over the Gentiles lord it over them, and their great men exercise authority over them. But it shall not be so among you; but whoever would be great among you must be your servant, and whoever must be first among you must be slave of all. For the Son of man came not to be served but to serve, and to give his life as a ransom for many.' (Mark 10:42–5)

It was the same message that Jesus gave to Philip and Andrew when they brought him the news that even the Gentiles were seeking him.

'He who loves his life loses it, and he who hates his life in this world will keep it for eternal life. If any one serves me, he must follow me; and where I am, there shall my servant be also; if any one serves me, the Father will honour him.' (John 12:25–6)

If there was anxiety among the disciples, it was a sensation to which Jesus himself was not immune. In his humanity he was tempted to take an easier path, to avoid the cross. It was truly the last temptation of Christ and it was with him to the end.

'Now is my soul troubled. And what shall I say? "Father, save me from this hour"? No, for this purpose I have come to this hour. Father, glorify thy name.' (John 12:27–8)

God's call is a call to service, whatever the cost. A group of orthodox Anglican clergy, fearing for the future in an increasingly heterodox Church, asked me if I thought they ought to keep a low profile. They were all comparatively young men, and were concerned that if they put their heads above the parapet they would for ever remain in the parishes where they now served. It was not an unreasonable fear and certainly there were dioceses where this would be so. I pointed out to them that it was easy for a priest approaching his sixty-fifth birthday (as I was) to tell them to stand up and be counted; and I warned them of the dangers of compromise. For a clergyman who has compromised his integrity is always a sorry creature, even when – especially when – it gains him the trappings of earthly advancement through clerical preferment. And I told them a cautionary tale.

Some years ago when I was still a parish priest, a young deacon, recently ordained and straight from theological college, came to me with a story of unseemly behaviour at his former seminary. The activities, which when I was a seminarian would have meant instant dismissal, were tacitly approved by the college principal. I had heard similar tales from two senior clergy whose word I trusted and I took up the matter at the highest level. I did not name the young man of course, and when I warned him that it may affect his future career, his reply was quick, courageous and to the point. 'I believe we must stand up for what is right, and I believe I must begin as I mean to go on.'

The fact that I raised it brought me an archbishop's rebuke. Then when the matter had been resolved satisfactorily (albeit reluctantly), attempts were made by the college authorities to prevent the young man's ordination to the priesthood, due that summer. His suffragan bishop, a good and godly man, interviewed him and told him he had been very courageous; but his diocesan bishop said he would never get another post in his diocese. He is now happily serving elsewhere as a school chaplain, teaching a generation of schoolboys about the things of God.

God may have a path for us which we cannot discern and it is not for those whom he calls to question it. On that first Palm Sunday, the anticipation was that Jesus would raise a conquering army and set up the reign of God upon earth. But he could pander to their expectations because his purpose was something else. So at the end of the day, after the excitement and tension, came the anticlimax. 'And he entered Jerusalem, and went into the temple; and when he had looked round at everything, as it was already late, he went out to Bethany with the twelve' (Mark 11:11).

By failing to fulfil the expectations they had of the Messiah and after raising their hopes to fever pitch, Jesus had sowed the seeds of his own destruction. Now there could be no turning back. It was the final onset of an inexorable journey which would end on the cross.

18

Cursing and Cleansing

St Mark's account of the week of the crucifixion places two events on the Monday, the cursing of the fig tree and the cleansing of the Temple. For St John, the cleansing takes place early in the ministry at another Passover feast, and its importance is that it did happen and not when it happened.

Roman coinage could not be used in the Temple precincts where the birds and animals for sacrifice were purchased, bearing as it did the image of the god-emperor. So booths were set up where, with the approval of the Temple authorities, money-changers provided a service to worshippers, changing the secular coins for those acceptable for use in the Temple. The exchange rate gave them a good discount and they were all the more unpopular for it.

Jesus' parents were devout believers who went every Passover to Jerusalem to keep the festival and Jesus would accompany them. We know that at the age of twelve he caused them great anxiety by staying behind.

After three days they found him in the temple, sitting among the teachers, listening to them and asking them questions; and all who heard him were amazed at his understanding and his answers. And when they saw him, they were astonished; and his mother said to him, 'Son, why have you treated us so? Behold, your father and I have been looking for you anxiously.' 'How is it that you sought me? Did you not know that I must be in my Father's house?' (Luke 2:46–9)

Maybe even so young, he was shocked at the babble of voices, the arguments, the cheating which took place in the house of God. At any rate we know that it was by no means his first sight of the noisy confusion when he took action against it, whether at the beginning or the end of his ministry. In either case it was a symbolic act at a moment deliberately chosen by him for maximum effect.

And he entered the temple and began to drive out those who sold and those who bought in the temple, and he overturned the tables of the money-changers and the seats of those who sold pigeons; and he would not allow anyone to carry anything through the temple. And he taught, and said to them, 'Is it not written, "My house shall be called a house of prayer for all nations"?' And the chief priests and the scribes heard it and sought a way to destroy him; for they feared him, because all the multitude was astonished at his teaching. (Mark 11:15–18)

In 1983, I was a delegate to an international ecumenical assembly in Vancouver. Among other events, there was every day a Bible study in small groups, and it was moving to study the Scriptures with people of every race and many different Christian denominations. In the group I attended there was a young Russian woman, a Baptist, who made occasional contributions but for much of the time listened quietly to the discussions. That is, until we began to speak of the Church, both buildings and people.

Someone made the obvious comment that the real Church of Christ is people and not buildings. At this, Valentina became quite agitated. 'Yes, yes, yes,' she said, in English with a heavy Russian accent. 'In my church, we understand this very well. Often we have had to worship deep in the forest.'

There was silence for a minute or so, as each of us pictured the Russian forest, perhaps in the snow, and this little Russian woman trudging through the undergrowth with her friends to a clearing in order to worship God. Anxious all the time in case they had been followed, fearful of a rush of soldiers with guns to break up their service, wondering if the day would end in a prison cell. It was the witness and the courage of millions of Valentinas which kept the faith alive in the dark days of Soviet oppression.

There is a place for discretion as there is a place for valour wherever the Church is under threat from the forces of secularism, be it in the obvious situation when Christians serve under a persecuting regime or in our own society where ridicule is more likely than active persecution, yet where the attractions of conformity to secular pressures must be faced by the Church. Discretion perhaps sometimes, valour certainly, but never, never, never must there be compromise. St Paul's words are as apt for life today in the democratic west as they were for Valentina as she faced all the dangers of Christian commitment in the Soviet Union. 'Be not conformed to this world but be transformed by the renewing of your mind, that you may prove what is the will of God, what is good and acceptable and perfect' (Romans 12:2).

But even though the Church is the people and not the buildings, we do have our places of worship, much loved, often magnificent and triumphant expressions of our awareness of the glory of God. And they are much loved and rightly so. As I visit the churches of my own archdeaconry, I know that there is not a single one which is neglected. Indeed they are probably in a better state of care and repair than at any time in their sometimes long history.

That care is in itself a recognition of their primary purpose in the worship of God. Some are eight, nine, even ten centuries old, some of them stone buildings erected on a site where once stood a wooden Saxon structure. Visit York Minster in whose foundations are the remains of the Roman basilica where Constantine was declared Emperor, one of the most significant events in Christian history; or St Michael-le-Belfry in York where Guy Fawkes was baptised; or Goodmanham, standing on the site of a pagan temple which was destroyed on the orders of its abbot when King Edwin was converted to Christianity in about AD 627; or many others, whose very stones have absorbed the prayers of the saints of many generations, of which we can surely say, 'This is none other than the house of God, this is the gate of heaven.'

To respect a place of worship for its purpose is to honour its holiness and to honour too the one in whose name it is used. When Jesus 'overturned the tables of the money-changers and the seats of those who sold pigeons', he was asserting the holiness of the house of God and, more widely, denouncing the secularism which can sometimes figuratively and sometimes literally seem to overturn the purposes of God.

At the time, it was moreover a popular action. The money-changers were known to cheat their customers and were little loved for it; while the devout could not but be offended at the spoliation of their holy place by the activities of the market-place. Again, as in his triumphal entry into the city on the previous day, he had the ordinary people behind him. And again he could, had he wished to fulfil their understanding of his Messiahship, have raised the army they hoped for to drive out the oppressors. But it was not his purpose. 'And when evening came, they went out of the city' (Mark 11:19).

As they were on the journey back to Bethany, they saw that a fig-tree, cursed by Jesus on the way into the city that morning, had withered. It is a strange story. It was not the season for figs, and it seems unreasonable that Jesus should have cursed a tree for not providing him with fruit to eat at a time of the year when it could not be expected to yield any fruit.

In such circumstances, we need to look behind the actuality to find the symbol, though he himself made no interpretation of its meaning. It may be that just as he was to cleanse the house of God of the impurities by which it was constantly defiled, the fig-tree without fruit stands for the house of Israel, also fruitless.

When Peter pointed out to Jesus that the fig-tree had withered, his response suggests that interpretation.

> And Jesus answered them, 'Have faith in God. Truly, I say to you, whoever says to this mountain, "Be taken up and cast into the sea," and does not doubt it in his heart, but believes that what he says will come to pass, it will be done for him. Therefore I tell you, whatever you ask in prayer, believe that you will receive it, and you will. And whenever you stand praying, forgive, if you have anything against any one; so that your Father also who is in heaven may forgive you your trespasses.' (Mark 11:22–5)

It is said that the idiom, 'mountain-remover' was commonly used to refer to those who could remove great difficulties. Thus a teacher who could explain difficult passages of Scripture was a 'mountain-remover'.

But taken as a whole the comments which Jesus made do point to the two aspects of Christian witness, the duty towards God and the duty towards one's neighbour. These are the two relationships which matter and for which Christ was to die on the cross. His sacrifice was to restore the broken relationship between man and God, broken that is by man's sin, by which we use our free will to choose not to serve God and do his will. But that relationship with God must be mirrored in our relations with those around us. He forgives us our sins in the same measure that 'we forgive those who sin against us'.

Yet it is more than a personal admonition, a withering of a fig-tree symbolising the decay our souls will suffer if we fail to respond to the grace which God freely offers to us. It is also a condemnation of the withered house of Israel, constantly compromising in its collaboration with the demands of pagan Rome. It is a warning to the Church of today not to collaborate with the siren voices which call it away from its true vocation to love the living God and serve him alone.

19

Questions and Answers

To the most serious of questions, there are no easy answers. Those of us who often face journalists know the problem only too well, for the sound-bite which they expect is to put into black and white that for which the only colour is grey. Moreover, from a five-minute conversation with an interviewer in which many shades of an argument may be expressed, the one sentence which makes for a good headline will be extracted. But better a sound-bite than silence, better a misunderstanding than a refusal to speak out for the truth.

It is not simply that those who speak controversially have a duty to respond to those who challenge what has been said, though that is certainly an obligation. It is an obligation to defend what one believes to be true, and in the process to be forced to examine the position one has taken, perhaps modifying it in the light of points which previously had been ignored. It is also an obligation to the truth itself, particularly when it is the truths of God which are at stake, and to be ready to face the ridicule or criticism or obloquy which is its reward. In any case for the Christian it is to follow in the steps of the Master.

In St Mark's chronology of Holy Week, Tuesday is the day on which Jesus once again came from Bethany where he was staying into Jerusalem. It was his last visit before his arrest, and he spent the day in disputation, challenging the very heart of religion which was presented by the ecclesiastical authorities.

In it, he showed a consummate skill which his enemies could not counter.

First there came the chief priests and scribes and elders, as he walked in the precincts of the Temple itself. There can be little doubt that they had spent long hours in the tense days since his arrival discussing how they might deal with him, how they might resist the threat to their position and their religion which he posed, not least in their fragile relationship with the secular authorities of Rome. At the heart of the problem was the origin of the authority which he affirmed by his actions and words.

> 'By what authority are you doing these things, or who gave you this authority to do them?' Jesus said to them, 'I will ask you a question; answer me, and I will tell you by what authority I do these things. Was the baptism of John from heaven or from men? Answer me.' (Mark 11:28–30)

It was a clever ploy, for the chief priests and their colleagues knew that whichever answer they gave, they were in trouble.

> And they argued with one another, 'If we say, "From heaven", he will say, 'Why then did you not believe him?' But shall we say, "From men"?' – they were afraid of the people, for all held that John was a real prophet. So they answered, 'We do not know.' And Jesus said to them, 'Neither will I tell you by what authority I do these things.' (Mark 11:31–3)

Then Jesus went on to the offensive, with a parable which was both a proclamation of his own authority and a challenge to theirs.

> A man planted a vineyard, and set a hedge around it, and dug a pit for the wine press, and built a tower, and let it out to tenants, and went to another country. (Mark 12:1)

From what followed it quickly became clear to his hearers,

the leaders of the Jewish religion, that the man who planted the vineyard was God Himself and the place, the land promised to Moses for the chosen people of Israel. The religious authorities were the tenants, given a charge by God to bring forth the fruits of his great and unique revelation. The owner of the vineyard from time to time sends servants for some of the fruits of the vineyard. These were the prophets of God, and when the first came,

> they took him and beat him, and sent him away empty-handed. Again he sent to them another servant, and they wounded him in the head and treated him shamefully. And he sent another, and him they killed; and so with many others, some they beat and some they killed. (Mark 12:3–5)

It tore at the core of their pride as servants of the living God; for the story of God's dealing with His people was a tale of their frequent and repeated rejection of His word and of their hardness of heart in the face of His prophets. But there was worse to come, as Jesus continued the parable.

> He had still one other, a beloved son; finally he sent him to them, saying, 'They will respect my son.' But those tenants said to one another, 'This is the heir; come, let us kill him, and the inheritance will be ours.' And they took him, and killed him, and cast him out of the vineyard. What will the owner of the vineyard do? He will come and destroy the tenants, and give the vineyard to others. Have you not read this scripture: 'The very stone which the builders rejected has become the head of the corner; this was the Lord's doing, and it is marvellous in our eyes'? (Mark 12:6–11)

He had turned the tables on them utterly and it was too much for them.

And they tried to arrest him, but feared the multitude, for

they perceived that he had told the parable against them; so
they left him and went away. (Mark 12:12)

In September 1620, a tiny ship left Amsterdam, calling at
London and Southampton. It was the *Mayflower*, and its
passengers, many fleeing from religious persecution, became
known as the Pilgrim Fathers. They formed the Plymouth
Settlement on the coast of New England across the Atlantic,
and survived many privations and hardships.

In our own time, a direct descendant of one of their leaders
had himself – ironically – suffered his own time of trial for
standing up for his beliefs. A priest of the Episcopal Church of
America, he became rector of a large parish in a New England
city. It had the third largest congregation in the diocese, with
a higher-than-average Afro-Caribbean membership. It was
traditional in its beliefs and in its worship, active with the poor
of the city, firm in its teaching of biblical doctrine and moral
standards. It refused to accept the ordination of women to the
priesthood or episcopate, and rejected the popular teaching that
practising homosexuals could be ordained or that single-sex
marriages could be solemnised.

Unfortunately for the rector of the parish, these were all
causes espoused not only by the Episcopal Church but by the
bishop of the diocese, who after a process which, it is said,
had little in it which conformed to the democratic standards
to which America aspires, finally issued a 'godly judgement'
depriving the priest of his rectorship (and as a result also of
his home).

In a less extreme form, similar persecution of loyal and
orthodox clergy is emerging in our own country. The judgment
of God, which Jesus sets out in the parable of the vineyard, will
be upon those Church leaders who initiate such action against
God's faithful servants, and upon those who fail to support or
defend them. The owner of the vineyard will come and destroy
the tenants, and give the vineyard to others.

To return to the Temple: after the chief priests and scribes
and elders had left Jesus, it was the turn of the Pharisees and

Herodians to challenge him. The Pharisees appear in the gospel stories as the main opponents of Jesus and his teaching, and to some degree this is a false picture. Certainly they attacked him because he claimed to forgive sins, and for breaking the Sabbath and mixing with sinners; and he denounced them in return for their many formal precepts which even they could not keep, and for their purely formal observance of the Law.

Yet the Pharisees were popular with the ordinary people, respected for their austere way of life and admired for their dislike both of the pagan rulers and of the priestly caste at the Temple whom they regarded as traitors who compromised and collaborated with the occupying forces. For a similar reason they were opponents of the Herodians, who were probably members of the family or caste of Herod and themselves collaborated with the Romans to retain their position.

On this occasion the Pharisees and Herodians came together to dispute with Jesus, but as opponents towards each other rather than as colleagues.

'Teacher, we know that you are true and care for no man; for you do not regard the position of men, but truly teach the way of God. Is it lawful to pay taxes to Caesar, or not? Should we pay them or not?' (Mark 12:14–15)

If he replied that it was indeed lawful to pay taxes to the pagan invaders, he could be branded as a collaborator himself; or if he declared it unlawful, they would be able to denounce him to the Roman authorities as a dangerous trouble-maker.

But knowing their hypocrisy, he said to them, 'Why put me to the test? Bring me a coin, and let me look at it.' And they brought one. And he said to them, 'Whose likeness and inscription is this?' They said to him, 'Caesar's.' Jesus said to them, 'Render to Caesar the things that are Caesar's, and to God the things that are God's.' And they were amazed at him. (Mark 12:15–17)

There is evidence that from this point onwards the Pharisees are more sympathetic towards Jesus, and certainly they would have supported that final statement, setting out the double duty and requirement, to serve God and to respect an earthly ruler. Another Pharisee, of the strictest sect of that group, who yet became the apostle Paul, was to direct later:

> Let every person be subject to the governing authorities. For there is no authority except from God, and those who exist have been instituted by God. Therefore he who resists the authorities resists what God has appointed, and those who resist will incur judgement. (Romans 13:1–2)

After the Pharisees came the Sadducees. If the Pharisees were the party of the common people, the Sadducees were that of the rich and powerful, unpopular with the masses but politically of great influence. In order to safeguard their own power and privilege, they were ready to compromise the purity of religious belief and practice. They opposed the strictness pursued by the Pharisees in doctrine and ethical standards, and were particularly known for their rejection of a belief in retribution in an after-life and in the resurrection of the body. They have their parallels in the modern Christian church, but disappeared from Judaism after the fall of Jerusalem in AD 70.

The question which they put to Jesus too has echoes of the supercilious treatment which orthodox believers sometimes experience in contemporary Christian debate, and there is a necessary firmness – almost harshness – in the manner of Jesus' response which is absent from the gentler sensitivity of his replies to Pharisees and Herodians, and even of those to the chief priests and scribes.

> And Sadducees came to him, who say there is no resurrection; and they asked him a question, saying, 'Teacher, Moses wrote for us that if a man's brother dies and leaves

a wife, but leaves no child, the man must take his wife, and raise up children for his brother. There were seven brothers; the first took a wife, and when he died left no children; and the second took her, and died, leaving no children; and the third likewise; and the seven left no children. Last of all the woman also died. In the resurrection whose wife shall she be? For the seven had her as wife.' (Mark 12:18–23)

Picture the group around Jesus, smirking, nudging one another: 'That's put this Galilean peasant in his place. And it's shown what a nonsense the idea of resurrection is.' Jesus is merciless in his response.

'Is not this why you are wrong, that you know neither the scriptures nor the power of God? For when they rise from the dead, they neither marry nor are given in marriage, but are like angels in heaven. As for the dead being raised, have you not read in the book of Moses, in the passage about the bush, how God said to him, "I am the God of Abraham, and the God of Isaac, and the God of Jacob"? He is not the God of the dead, but of the living; you are quite wrong.' (Mark 12:24–7)

'You know neither the scriptures nor the power of God'.
'. . . *when* they rise from the dead . . .'
'. . . are like the angels in heaven . . .' (The Sadducees also rejected the existence of angels.) 'You are quite wrong.' – it would have been quite an experience to hear Jesus in a modern Christian assembly, answering a debate in which bishops and theologians had laboured to deny basic teachings of the Christian creeds.

In the Temple, the mood changed. He had defeated the challenge of the chief priests and scribes and elders, and had silenced the Sadducees, popular moves with the ordinary people; and he had answered the dispute between the Pharisee and Herodian positions in a manner which had satisfied the

Pharisees – who from then on were never again his major
enemies. Indeed it was Gamaliel, one of their number, who
publicly defended the apostles before the Sanhedrin.

After Jesus had dealt so firmly with the Sadducees, one
of the scribes, who had seen 'that he answered them well',
asked him,

'Which commandment is the first of all?' Jesus answered,
'The first is, "Hear, O Israel: the Lord our God is one; and
you shall love the Lord your God with all your heart, and
with all your soul, and with all your mind, and with all your
strength." The second is this, "You shall love your neighbour
as yourself." There is no commandment greater than these.'
(Mark 12:28–33)

It is a three-fold command: to love God, to love one's
neighbour, *and to love oneself*. To love God with all one's
heart is to love Him with the emotions, as one would love a
friend or a spouse. It is the love which is based in total loyalty,
absolute trust, in the certain knowledge that it is a relationship
of utter and complete fidelity.

To love God with all one's soul is to love Him with the
totality of the person, to know that unity with Him which
is like the oneness of husband and wife, where the coming
together in marriage is the mathematical impossibility of one
plus one equalling one, yet where the sum is greater than the
two parts of which it is composed.

To love God with all one's mind is to know that it is
intellectually reasonable to love a divine being who revealed
Himself in Jesus Christ and so loved the world that He gave
His only son to die on the cross to save us from our sins and
restore us to that relationship with Him which is His purpose
for us. 'Whoever confesses that Jesus is the Son of God, God
abides in him, and he in God. So we know and believe the
love God has for us' (I John 4:15–16).

To love him with all our strength is to love him so fully that
we are ready to devote ourselves to his service, unconditionally

and without question. 'By this we know love, that he laid down his life for us; and we ought to lay down our lives for the brethren' (1 John 3:16).

To love our neighbour is to love that which God Himself loves, however difficult or unlikely or unreciprocated that love may appear to be.

> If any one says, 'I love God,' and hates his brother, he is a liar; for he who does not love his brother whom he has seen, cannot love God whom he has not seen. (1 John 4:20)

> Beloved, let us love one another; for love is of God, and he who loves is born of God and knows God. (1 John 4:7)

But we are also to love ourselves, for the commandment we have been given is quite specific. 'You shall love your neighbour as yourself.' Can this really be? Is not self-love to be rejected as selfishness, in other words to be resisted as a sin? Yet we are people whom God loves – men, women and children, sinful, disobedient, spiteful, sometimes hateful, in whom God can see something to love.

It is not simply that we should fulfil the command of Jesus (Luke 6:31), 'As you wish that men would do to you, do so to them'; nor even the more limited requirement that we pray that our sins be forgiven in the same measure that we forgive the sins of others. It is a positive requirement that we love ourselves; and we need to meditate on its meaning for each of us.

The scribe who had asked Jesus which commandment was the first of all responded enthusiastically to his reply.

> 'You are right, Teacher; you have truly said that he is one, and there is no other but he; and to love him with all the heart, and with all the understanding, and with all the strength, and to love one's neighbour as oneself, is much more than all whole burnt offerings and sacrifices.' And when Jesus saw that he answered wisely, he said to him,

'You are not far from the kingdom of God.' And after that no one dared to ask him any question. (Mark 12:32–4)

For a time that day, he remained in the Temple, teaching a little, watching, waiting. It was to be his final visit to Jerusalem before his arrest. Now he could come and go as he wished; when he returned, he would be in the hands and the power of others who would take him out and crucify him by the city gates.

20

Trials and Tribulations

On leaving the city, he rested for a time on the Mount of Olives with Peter, James and John, his inner circle of most trusted followers. The warnings which he gave are warnings for Christians for all time, and speak for themselves, as recorded by St Mark.

> Take heed that no one leads you astray. Many will come in my name, saying, 'I am he!' and they will lead many astray. And when you hear of wars and rumours of wars, do not be alarmed; this must take place, but the end is not yet. For nation will rise against nation, and kingdom against kingdom; there will be earthquakes in various places, there will be famines; this is but the beginning of sufferings. (Mark 13:5–8)

The world is little changed since that day on which Jesus issued his dire warning. If the great wars which rent Europe asunder are no more, there is even now never a time when the world is totally at peace. The terrible slaughter of the Holocaust, with the horrors of Auschwitz and Buchenwald and Belsen and the rest is at an end; but not the destruction of the Kurdish people, nor the genocide in Bosnia.

A few years ago, I was due to attend a conference in Los Angeles when a severe earthquake shook the city and there were fears that this would be the prelude to the Big One

which scientists predict will one day engulf the West Coast
of America. I set off in some trepidation.

As the aircraft came in to land at Los Angeles, someone
pointed out a burning building below us. Then there was
another, and another, several major fires burning below us
in the city. We were over-flying South Central Los Angeles
and it was the beginning of the riots of 1992 – earthquakes,
riots, murders: I thought of the warnings our Lord gave on the
Mount of Olives. But even in all the conflict and murderous
mayhem, there was hope.

There was constant live television news coverage, which
I watched in between conference commitments. A white
policeman approached one cameraman. 'Don't think the folk
of South Central are all like this,' he said, pointing to the
looters and to the burning shops and offices. 'Most folk here
are decent and law-abiding.' Another newsman saw a large
crowd approaching and stayed at his post, though some white
men had been beaten and murdered. As the crowd came nearer,
he realised with relief that they were carrying not weapons, but
shovels and brooms to begin clearing the broken glass and trash
covering the streets and supermarket floors.

Then there was the crowd outside a Korean shop (the
Koreans had suffered racial violence from the predominantly
black rioters and many shops had been looted and burned).
There was an elderly grey-haired white man, several Hispanics,
a couple of Koreans and a large black man who took it upon
himself to be spokesman to the journalist. 'Why are we here?
Why, to stop them doing to this shop what they've done to
those a block away. This man's a decent man and we've come
to protect him.' He added with a broad grin, 'And anyway he's
got my best suit in for cleaning, and I ain't gonna let them take
it away.'

Earlier that year I had been in South Africa, still suffering
under the yoke of apartheid. Fifteen years before, I had walked
after dark in the centre of Johannesburg, visiting the cinema
and returning alone to my hotel. This time the streets were
empty for fear, and full of fear. The houses where I stayed were

fortresses with high walls and security gates, with warnings of 'immediate armed response' if they were attacked. Yet there was hope too, and an awareness – not there on my previous visit – that apartheid was an evil which must be removed, as it now has been.

The Cold War between East and West is past history, though peace has yet to break out in parts of the old Soviet Union. Yet as one threat to world peace was removed, another arose to take its place in the emergence of militant Islam and the imperial aspirations of Iraq's leaders.

> But take heed to yourselves; for they will deliver you up to the councils; and you will be beaten in synagogues; and you will stand before governors and kings for my sake, to bear testimony before them. And the gospel must first be preached to all nations. And when they bring you to trial and deliver you up, do not be anxious beforehand what you will say; but say whatever is given you in that hour, for it is not you who speak, but the Holy Spirit. (Mark 13:9–11)

The prophecy was not only of natural disaster and internecine conflict: there was to be conflict too within the faith. The followers of Christ were first persecuted by the religious authorities, and it was only a short time before the prophetic warning was fulfilled with a vengeance. But God is with those who seek to serve him regardless of the pain and ridicule inflicted by those who oppose. It is hardest when it comes from those who might be thought to be fellow-believers, as those of us who have stood for the truths of scripture in what often seems to be a post-Christian Church know only too well.

> And brother will deliver up brother to death, and the father his child, and children will rise against parents and have them put to death; and you will be hated by all for my name's sake. But he who endures to the end will be saved.

Whatever the cost and whatever the pain, the victory has

already been won by Jesus on the cross. My own experience
has often been a painful one, but it is as nothing when I think
of the pain I would have endured if I had chosen the common
path of compromise or silence.

> But when you see the desolating sacrilege set up where it
> ought not to be (let the reader understand), then let those
> who are in Judea flee to the mountains; let him who is on the
> housetop go not down, nor enter his house to take anything
> away; and let him who is in the field not turn back to take his
> mantle. And alas for those who are with child and for those
> who give suck in those days! Pray that it may not happen in
> winter. For in those days there will be such tribulation as
> has not been from the beginning of the creation which God
> created until now, and never will be. And if the Lord had not
> shortened the days, no human being would be saved; but for
> the sake of the elect, whom he chose, he shortened the days.
> And then if anyone says to you, 'Look, here is the Christ!'
> or 'Look, there he is!' do not believe it. False Christs and
> false prophets will arise and show signs and wonders, to lead
> astray, if it were possible, the elect. But take heed; I have
> told you these things beforehand. (Mark 13:14–23)

Today, in many parts of the Church – not only the Anglican
Church world-wide, but our sister churches too – alien teaching
is spreading like a cancer, false prophets and teachers who
would indeed lead astray the elect of God. Biblical revelation is
watered down, God's moral absolutes are replaced by a secular
relativism which destroys the reality of the Good News which
Jesus brought, and even the liturgy of the Church, in which
what we pray should be that which we believe, is polluted by
New Age and feminist principles which overturn the unique
revelation of God which first came to the people of the Jews.
    There are times when I am near despair at what has happened
to a Church I have served for over forty years. But despair is
wrong. For it is God's Church and we have His promise that
even the gates of hell shall not prevail against it. In the end,

His truth will triumph as it has always done in the dark days of apostasy throughout history. Our task is simply to recognise that it was for this time that He first called us; and that our only duty is to remain faithful, however dark the skies may become.

But in those days, after that tribulation, the sun will be darkened, and the moon will not give its light, and the stars will be falling from heaven, and the powers in the heavens will be shaken. And then they will see the Son of Man coming in clouds with great power and glory. And then he will send out the angels, and gather his elect from the four winds, from the ends of the earth to the ends of heaven.

From the fig tree learn its lesson: as soon as its branch becomes tender and puts forth its leaves, you know that summer is near. So also, when you see these things taking place, you know that he is near, at the very gates. Truly, I say to you, this generation will not pass away before all these things take place. Heaven and earth will pass away, but my words will not pass away. (Mark 13:24–31)

We need no other support than that assurance. With it, we know that the Shepherd will be with us, even when we walk in the valley of the shadow of death. For we know neither the day nor the hour when the trials will come, nor when His victory will be proclaimed and He will take the Church back to Himself.

But of that day or that hour no one knows, not even the angels in heaven, nor the Son, but only the Father. Take heed, watch; for you do not know when the time will come. It is like a man going on a journey, when he leaves home and puts his servants in charge, each with his work, and commands the door-keeper to be on the watch. Watch therefore – for you do not know when the master of the house will come, in the evening, or at midnight, or at cockcrow, or in the morning – lest he come suddenly and find you asleep. And what I say to you I say to all: Watch. (Mark 13:32–7)

But this I know, the skies will fill with rapture,
and myriad, myriad human voices sing,
and earth to heaven, and heaven to earth, will answer:
At last the Saviour, Saviour of the world, is King!

21

Wine and Water

There is, as the Preacher says, 'a time to keep silence, and a time to speak', 'a time for war, and a time for peace'. 'For everything there is a season and a time for every matter under heaven' (Ecclesiastes 3:7, 8 and 1). After the tension of the day of the triumphal entry into Jerusalem, after the babble and noise of the day of the cleansing, after the turmoil of the day of questions and answers, there was a need for calm before the final storm.

So on the day before the last supper together with his disciples and two days before the Passover festival, Jesus rested in Bethany with his friends. St Mark places the anointing in the house of Simon the leper on this day rather than earlier as in St John's account (see chapter 18). I have taken John's chronology because I believe his to be the eye-witness gospel record, though it makes little difference. Mark does suggest that it was at this later point that Judas 'went to the chief priests in order to betray him to them. And when they heard it they were glad, and promised to give him money. And he sought an opportunity to betray him' (Mark 14:10–11).

Judas was the intellectual in the little group of twelve apostles chosen by Jesus. This is not to fall into the modern trap of upholding the rest of the twelve as poor working men, examples of the affirmation by Jesus of the poor and dispossessed. Peter, Andrew, James and John were middle-class entrepreneurs, sons of father with a fishing business which was sufficiently prosperous for the boys to take leave to be with Jesus on his journeyings. They were not illiterate peasants; but they were not at the academic level of a Judas Iscariot.

Judas was not only the treasurer, able to keep the books and look after the little money which the group needed for subsistence; he was also the thinker, the one who 'really knew' what Messiahship meant. We can speculate that either he became so disillusioned that Jesus was not fulfilling the picture which Judas held of the role of the Messiah that he must be stopped in his tracks before further damage was done; or that the offer to betray Jesus was a devious (and misguided) plan to force him into the open and guide him along a track which Jesus was apparently reluctant to take.

Either possibility could explain his eventual suicide after the crucifixion, on the one scenario that he sought only his arrest and removal from the scene (since the religious authorities had, on their own admission, no power of execution); on the other that the plan had failed in utter disaster, and that he had betrayed the one to whom he had complete devotion.

Perhaps Jesus spent the long day of rest in Bethany in prayer, agonising about what was to come. The next day, it was time for action, and as with the triumphal entry on the day we call Palm Sunday, so with the Last Supper on our Maundy Thursday, Jesus had made careful and secret preparations. It was their custom to keep the Passover in Jerusalem itself, but it was a dangerous place now for Jesus. When the disciples asked where they were to go in the city to prepare for Passover, he took two of them aside privately.

'Go into the city, and a man carrying a jar of water will meet you; follow him, and wherever he enters, say to the householder, "The Teacher says, Where is my guest room, where I am to eat the Passover with my disciples?" And he will show you a large upper room furnished and ready; there prepare for us.' (Mark 14:13–15)

It has all the marks of a clandestine operation: a man, known and trusted by Jesus but not known to the two disciples, who had been told to look out for them in the crowds thronging the city. Maybe he knew them by sight, maybe not, but as he walked around, he would be easy to pick out carrying a pitcher of water, since this was not normally a man's task. As soon as he was conscious that he was being followed, he was to lead them to a particular house. He would enter, they would follow, and he would probably then leave, perhaps unknown to the householder.

He too would be a follower of Jesus but again not known to the two disciples. He had to be sure that these were the people of whom Jesus had spoken, and the password was demanded and given: 'The Teacher says, Where is the guest room where I am to eat the Passover with my disciples?' There they would remain, preparing the meal and ritual requirements, so that all would be ready when Jesus arrived under the safety of darkness.

Unlike the Gospels of St Matthew, Mark and Luke, St John has no record of the institution of the Lord's Supper (see chapter 6), but he does record an incident ignored by the other evangelists, in that sublimity of descriptive language which sets his account apart.

> Jesus, knowing that the Father had given all things into his hands, and that he had come from God and was going to God, rose from supper, laid aside his garments, and girded himself with a towel. Then he poured water into a basin, and began to wash the disciples' feet, and to wipe them with the towel with which he was girded. (John 13:3–6)

As always, Simon Peter got it wrong and asked defensively, 'Surely you aren't going to wash my feet?' If there was any mark of respect and honour to be accorded, surely it was, in Peter's mind, for him to wash the Master's feet. 'I won't let you do it.'

Jesus told him, gently, 'If I do not wash your feet, you have no part in me.' That would be unthinkable, and Peter responded with his usual unbridled enthusiasm, 'In that case, not only my feet but my head and hands as well!'

A smile played on the lips of Jesus as, kneeling, he looked up into Peter's eyes. 'That really won't be necessary, Peter.'

> 'He who has bathed does not need to wash, except for his feet, but he is clean all over; and you are clean, but not all of you.' (John 13:10)

After the feet-washing, Jesus explained its meaning, and once again emphasised that to be a disciple of Christ is to follow a pattern of servanthood set by the Lord himself. It is a teaching we cannot hear often enough.

> 'You call me Teacher and Lord; and you are right, for so I am. If I then, your Lord and Teacher, have washed your feet, you also ought to wash one another's feet. For I have given you an example, that you should do as I have done to you. Truly, truly, I say to you, a servant is not greater than his master; nor is he who is sent greater than he who sent him. If you know these things, blessed are you if you do them.' (John 13:13–17)

He had warned them that not all were trustworthy, in that chilling phrase, 'You are clean – but not all of you.' I had once inadvertently betrayed a confidence, and this was raised at the meeting where the confidential information had been shared with members. The chairman commented, accusingly, 'It has to be someone sitting round this table.' I tried not to look guilty, but the guilt was there, even though it had not been a deliberate betrayal and even though I had thought I was acting for the best and with propriety. I remained silent during the meeting and apologised afterwards privately to the chairman, who was very understanding.

Whatever motive Judas might have had for his talks with the chief priests, he could not but have felt deeply uneasy under the knowing, penetrating gaze of Jesus. The other disciples were clearly not aware of the traitor's identity, and each was concerned who it might be. As they sought to identify betrayal in another, each would be searching his own conscience and fearing for his own strength.

> One of the disciples, whom Jesus loved, was lying close to the breast of Jesus; so Simon Peter beckoned to him and said, 'Tell us who it is of whom he speaks.' So lying thus, close to the breast of Jesus, he said to him, 'Lord, who is it?' Jesus answered, 'It is he to whom I shall give this morsel when I have dipped it.' So when he had dipped the morsel, he gave it to Judas, the son of Simon Iscariot. Then after the morsel, Satan entered into him. Jesus said to him, 'What you are going to do, do quickly.' (John 13:23–7)

Why did John not expose the traitor? Perhaps because the giving of a dipped morsel was a common enough act of hospitality within the ritual of a meal, it was one among many such dippings. Or maybe at that time, it was unthinkable to John that Judas of all people could be the traitor. It is hard for us at a distance of two millennia and of another culture to understand exactly how such ritual was conducted or even the body language of the participants, familiar to them but utterly hidden from us.

Even today, different cultures have varieties of such rituals. My wife and I were once present at a dinner party in Sweden where it is (or was then) customary for the hostess to honour each guest, one at a time, by raising her glass, saying 'Skoll' and drinking. The guest must then respond similarly and guest and hostess both drink. At a large gathering, it is difficult in the extreme for a hostess to remain sober.

Whatever the reason, the instruction which Jesus gave to Judas, 'What you are going to do, do quickly', was not remarked upon by any other present, not even by John.

> Now no one at the table knew why he said this to him. Some thought that, because Judas had the money box, Jesus was

telling him, 'Buy what we need for the feast'; or that he should give something to the poor. So, after receiving the morsel, he immediately went out; *and it was night*. (John 13:28–30)

'And it was night': in that dramatic phrase is encapsulated the nature of the battle in which Jesus was engaged; between light and darkness, between good and evil, between everlasting life and eternal death. Yet it is a battle whose outcome was foreshadowed by the triumphant proclamation by Jesus which followed and by the departure of the traitor into the night.

Now is the Son of Man glorified, and in him God is glorified; if God is glorified in him, God will also glorify him in himself, and glorify him at once' (John 13:31–2)

In the sublime introduction to St John's Gospel, the evangelist speaks of Jesus as the one who was in the beginning with God, who indeed was God, the Word made Flesh. 'In him was life and the life was the light of men. And the light shines in the darkness, and the darkness has not overcome it' (John 1:4–5).

Archbishop William Temple (in *Readings in St John's Gospel*, Macmillan, 1939, 1955) suggests that the last phrase should be translated 'the darkness did not absorb it'. Temple asks us to imagine standing alone on some headland on a dark night.

At the foot of the headland is a lighthouse or beacon, not casting its rays on every side, but throwing one bar of light through the darkness. It is some such image that St John had before his mind. The divine light shines through the darkness of the world, cleaving it, but neither despelling it nor quenched by it. (*Readings in St John's Gospel*, p. 7)

Temple can say this because, like us, he knows the end of the story. In Bach's *Mass in B minor*, the *Crucifixus* dies away in a desolation of emptiness and pain, as the one who was to be the Saviour of the world suffers death on the cross and is buried. It is all over, finished, no more dreams, no more visions of glory. The diminuendo gives way to a brief silence. Then, in a triumphant fanfare, *Et resurrexit*, he who was dead is risen, there is life not death, everlasting hope in place of utter despair. So Jesus can cap the desolate withdrawal of Judas, those terrible words 'and it was night', with the jubilant 'Now is the Son of Man glorified', confident in the power of God in which he shares.

Yet it was a real battle. Fully human and fully divine, Jesus has the power to sin, to deny the ground of his own being, to reject the very purpose for which he came, as surely as any one of us who share his humanity. If that were not so, he would not be truly human. That was the terrifying gamble which God took when the Word became flesh to dwell among us.

Soon that 'dwelling' would come to an end, at any rate in a physical sense, and after the departure of Judas, Jesus warned them that he was soon to leave, that where he was going, they could not come. For Simon Peter, brave, impulsive, self-confident Peter there is a particular warning.

> Simon Peter said to him, 'Lord, where are you going?' Jesus answered, 'Where I am going you cannot follow me now; but you shall follow hereafter.' Peter said to him, 'Lord, why cannot I follow you now? I will lay down my life for you.' Jesus answered, 'Will you lay down your life for me? Truly, truly, I say to you, the cock will not crow, till you have denied me three times.' (John 13:36–8)

Poor Peter, crushed again, left wondering if it was he who by some dreadful mistake would betray the Master he loved. But Jesus knew he not only needed that cautionary warning, but more important that he could cope with its implications. 'Don't worry how you are, how you will be – there is a place for all of you.'

Let not your hearts be troubled; believe in God, believe also

in me. In my Father's house are many rooms; if it were not
so, would I have told you that I go to prepare a place for you?
And when I go and prepare a place for you, I will come again
and will take you to myself, that where I am you may be also.
And you know the way I am going.' (John 14:1–4)

They naturally confused the temporal and spatial with the
eternal. Thomas expressed their bewilderment.

'Lord, we do not know where you are going; how can we
know the way?' Jesus said to him, 'I am the way, and the
truth, and the life; no one comes to the Father but by me.'
(John 14:5–6)

I find comfort in the very normality, the ordinariness of the
disciples. These are not plaster saints, but men and women,
young as well as old, who share my faults, my failures, my
misunderstandings, my sins, my arrogances, my bewilderment,
even though they have the advantage of the presence with
them of the living Jesus. Yet so do I, if not in the same
physical sense.

I have deliberately not talked of the Last Supper, though
this was the major event of the day we call Maundy Thursday,
because I have written of it elsewhere (chapter 6). But it is the
central fact of my spiritual life, for it is the focus of the presence
of Jesus whose promise is that he is with his people 'to the
close of the age' (Matthew 28:20). So it has been for Christians
down the ages, since that quiet meal in the upper room on the
day before the crucifixion. 'Do this in remembrance of me,'
said Jesus and his followers have done it always since then,
day after day.

For forty years or more, I have done it, as a priest or as a
communicant – in great cathedrals with a Mozart Mass and
orchestra and a vast congregation; in a country church with
four other worshippers; in a lecture room at the London School
of Economics; in a vast marquee in Vancouver and Canberra;
in a tiny church with open walls and chickens about the feet

in the Argentinian Chaco; with a multi-lingual congregation in the heat of southern Brazil; in an old church hall in Eaton Bray on Christmas Day; in a Lutheran Church in Wisconsin, a Presbyterian cathedral in Edinburgh; in more places than I can remember. No-one has expressed it better than the great liturgical scholar, Dom Gregory Dix, in *Shape of the Liturgy* (Dacre Press, 1945, p. 744):

Was ever another command so obeyed? For century after century, spreading slowly to every continent and country and among every race on earth, this action has been done, in every conceivable human circumstance, for every conceivable human need from infancy and before it to extreme old age and after it, from the pinnacles of earthly greatness to the refuge of fugitives in the caves and dens of the earth. Men have found no better thing than this to do

for kings at their crowning and for criminals going to the scaffold;

for armies in triumph or for a bride and bridegroom in a little country church;

for the proclamation of a dogma or for a good crop of wheat;

for the wisdom of Parliament or a mighty nation or for a sick old woman afraid to die;

for a schoolboy sitting an examination;

for Columbus setting out to discover America;

for the famine of whole provinces or for the soul of a dead lover;

in thankfulness because my father did not die of pneumonia;

for a village headman much tempted to return to fetish because the yams had failed;

because the Turk was at the gates of Vienna;

for the repentance of Margaret;

for the settlement of a strike;

for a son for a barren woman;

for Captain so-and-so, wounded and prisoner of war;

while lions roared in the amphitheatre;

on the beach at Dunkirk;

while the hiss of scythes in the thick June grass came faintly
through the windows of the church;

tremulously, by an old monk on the fiftieth anniversary of
his vows;

furtively, by an exiled bishop who had hewn timber all day
in a prison camp near Murmansk;

gorgeously, for the canonisation of St Joan of Arc

– one could fill many pages with the reasons why men have
done this, and not tell a hundredth part of them.

And best of all, week by week and month by month,
on a hundred thousand successive Sundays, faithful,
unfailingly, across all the parishes of Christendom, the
pastors have done this just to *make* the *plebs sancta Dei*
– the holy common people of God.

'Go in peace to love and serve the Lord' is the dismissal
sentence in the modern Anglican liturgy. So after the disciples
in the upper room had shared the bread and the wine which is
the sacramental Body and Blood of the Lord Jesus Christ, they
sang a hymn and left the city for the Mount of Olives. It was
near the end. They left in a tense peace and would surely love
and serve the Lord in the hours to come.

22

Agony and Arrest

The view of Jerusalem from the Garden of Gethsemane has changed much since the time when Jesus prayed there with his disciples. Gone is the great and beautiful Temple, and in its place Islam's golden Dome of the Rock. But the walk from the city across the Kidron valley to the slopes of the Mount of Olives opposite the city walls would be recognisable to the disciples today. The garden too remains a place of peace and tranquillity with its ancient, gnarled trees which some say have survived for two thousand years.

I found it to be one of the most evocative of all the sites of the Holy Land. To pray in the church, with its blue-glassed windows mimicking the darkness of the night, is to pray with Jesus himself as he agonised over what he knew was to come. This is particularly so in the chancel, where, surrounded by the altar rails, is an area of bare rock which is venerated as the very place where Jesus prayed on that last night. We cannot know if it is genuinely that spot, but to pray there is a deeply moving spiritual experience. In any event, Gethsemane was a place where Jesus often prayed with his disciples, and Judas himself was sufficiently confident that he would rest there for a time with them, before the ten-minute climb to the top of the Mount of Olives and then down to the village where he had been staying.

The agony of Jesus in Gethsemane was the climax of the temptation with which he had struggled throughout his ministry. From the earliest days of the ministry, there was forever the enticement to turn away from his true purpose and calling, and it was to be with him even on the cross.

After his baptism in the Jordan, he retreated for forty days of prayer and fasting in the wilderness, 'tempted by the devil' (Luke 4:2). The first temptation was to misuse his power for personal satisfaction, and Jesus met the temptation with a word of God.

> The devil said to him, 'If you are the Son of God, command this stone to become bread.' And Jesus answered him, 'It is written, "Man shall not live by bread alone."' (Luke 4:3–4)

I cannot speak for the laity of the Church who will have their own temptations which would draw them away from the service of Christ. But I do know the temptations which come to ordained clergy and ministers. One of the most distressing of the arguments employed in the debates on the ordination of women were from those (only a few, I suspect) who claimed the right to 'share in the power' which came with ordination to the priesthood. What power? A priest is always to be a servant of the servants of God, and there is nothing in the Gospels to suggest otherwise – and much to confirm it.

When we priests or ministers use power over another, it is always to the detriment of our priestliness, whether in 'pulling rank' through an acceptance of the hierarchical position which others may wish to confer upon us, or in the abuse of relationships for our own comfort or satisfaction. When we seek thus to turn stones into bread, we only succeed in turning the bread of God into stone.

The second temptation in the wilderness was also about power, about the assumption of earthly glory in place of heavenly kingship.

And the devil took him up, and showed him all the kingdoms

of the world in a moment of time, and said to him, 'To you I will give all this authority and their glory; for it has been delivered to me, and I give it to whom I will. If you, then, will worship me, it shall all be yours.' And Jesus answered him, 'It is written, "You shall worship the Lord your God, and him only shall you serve."' (Luke 4:5–8)

A retired colonel once approached me at a gathering. 'Young nephew of mine wants to become a parson. Can't understand why!' he told me in a voice suffused with incredulity. 'But he comes from a good family, went to a good school and so on, well-spoken, not over-bright but bright enough for a parson, and I want to help him if I can. Now he's obviously just the right material to be a bishop one day. What I want to ask you is how he should best go about getting there.'

There was no point in trying to explain that this was not what was meant by a call to the priesthood, and anyway I had met enough clergy who had set their sights on the purple from the very day of their ordination. So I answered as well as I could, not dishonestly but with a certain cynicism born of experience.

'Well,' I said, 'he's obviously started in the right way, with the poise and accent that a public school education would give him. He will have to read for a degree, but make sure it isn't in theology or philosophy. If he's to the left in his politics, perhaps Social Science would be a possibility, but he must make sure that his political radicalism is allowed to take charge over his religious convictions.'

The colonel assured me in a slightly horrified voice that his nephew was certainly not of the political left, 'nor is he one of those dreadful happy-clappies.' 'In that case,' I went on, 'he must make sure he goes to the right theological college. I suggest Cuddesdon or Westcott House, Cambridge, as they're the ecclesiastical equivalent of membership of the Athenaeum. He'll have to serve in a parish but tell him to choose his first vicar with care – someone who is likely to become a bishop himself. Agree with everything he says and make him feel he is important. It would be preferable after the first curacy if your nephew tried to get a non-parochial post, or become an expert in something – not social responsibility if he isn't left wing, maybe liturgy. Above all, he must look for the fashionable trends and support them publicly. Such things as gay marriage and calling God 'mother.' The colonel had gone rather pale by this time, and said he would try to put his nephew off the church after all.

An elaboration of what I actually said, turning into fantasy; but near enough to the reality of the ambitious priest's aspirations as to be deeply worrying, for integrity is the first casualty of ambition.

The third temptation was to the gimmickry which would have removed faith and replaced it with certainty. And now the devil used Scripture to his own ends.

> And he took him to Jerusalem, and set him upon the pinnacle of the temple, and said to him, 'If you are the Son of God, throw yourself down from here; for it is written, "He will give his angels charge over you, to guard you," and "On their hands they shall bear you up, lest you hurt your foot against a stone."' And Jesus answered him, 'It is said, "You shall not tempt the Lord your God."' (Luke 4:9–12)

There is a fine balance between, on the one hand, making the gospel relevant to those who need its message, by the use of new methods of worship, teaching and music, and, on the other, hiding the challenge of that message behind that which is superficially attractive. There is some truth in the saying, 'Any fool can fill a church, but it takes a saint to empty one.'

Jesus was tempted to misuse his powers to compel those he had come to save to accept his message, but to do so would have meant that he would gain followers not because they had heard and accepted the good news of the gospel, but because they had seen the wonders he had done. That was not his way, and again and again when he worked miracles, he begged those whom he had healed for compassion's sake to keep quiet about what he had done. There is no merit in believing because we cannot but believe; true faith comes when we cannot fully comprehend but yet believe and trust in the one who brought the message.

It would be mistaken to imagine that temptation came to Jesus only in the forty days in the wilderness, or in Gethsemane, or on the cross. The temptations were constant, and in every way that we have been tempted, so was he. 'For we have not a high priest who is unable to sympathise with our weaknesses, but one who *in every respect* has been tempted as we are, yet without sinning (Hebrews 4:11).

Above all, there was the temptation to avoid that for which he had come, the dreadful suffering and death on the cross. In Gethsemane he prayed agonisingly for just that, but also that God's will might be done.

> And when he came to the place he said to them, 'Pray that you may not enter into temptation.' And he withdrew from them about a stone's throw, and knelt down and prayed, 'Father, if thou art willing, remove this cup from me; nevertheless not my will, but thine, be done.' And there appeared to him an angel from heaven, strengthening him. And being in an agony he prayed more earnestly; and his sweat became like great drops of blood falling down upon the ground. (Luke 22:41–4)

It remained with him on the cross, when his enemies mocked him.

> And those who passed by derided him, wagging their heads, and saying, 'Aha! You who would destroy the temple and build it in three days, save yourself, and come down from the cross!' So also the chief priests mocked him to one another with the scribes, saying, 'He saved others; he cannot save himself. Let the Christ, the King of Israel, come down now from the cross, that we may see and believe.' (Mark 15:29–32)

It is a pity that the film, *The Last Temptation of Christ*, gave the impression that his last great temptation was that of lust for Mary Magdalene. In the film, the devil (in the shape of a well-spoken little English girl) persuades him to come down from the cross. He does so, marries Mary of Magdala, and raises a family. Later in life, with his family around him, Jesus is visited by Peter and a group of now-elderly disciples. Peter tells him, in a sad voice, that he spoiled everything by coming down from the cross – and he is back there, dying. It was all a dream, but a dream – a nightmare almost – of what would have been lost had he succumbed to that all-pervading and final temptation.

In Gethsemane, Jesus awoke to find that Peter, James and John had fallen asleep. In his agony, he had been quite alone.

One day in the Holy Land, we had taken a bus along the old, bumpy road from Jerusalem to Jericho, away from the modern metalled highway which takes a newer and lower route. We stopped for a while above the valley where the 'city of palm trees' lies, to listen to biblical accounts of the storming of old Jericho by Joshua, and of Jesus and Zacchaeus in the Jericho of New Testament days.

Suddenly we saw below in the valley and coming up the road towards us, still a mile or more away, what seemed to be a large crowd moving purposefully. In the Holy Land there is always a cautious tension, especially in the Arab West Bank territories, and some of our party had been stoned while walking through the Old City. It was certainly not just a few folk, by the swirling cloud of dust which was being raised from the rough, sandy road. A man leading the group was certainly carrying a stick. Just as we were preparing to climb back on the bus to beat a hasty retreat, one of our party, who had a pair of binoculars, trained them on the 'mob'. Then he laughed. It was a shepherd or goatherd leading his flock to pasture.

The air is clear in the Holy Land, and as Jesus talked with the sleepy disciples in Gethsemane, perhaps one would interrupt with the news that, across the Kidron valley, could be seen clearly the lights of torches, and a noise of shuffling, tramping feet and the babble of voices.

So Judas, procuring a band of soldiers and some officers from the chief priests and the Pharisees, went there with lanterns and torches and weapons. Then Jesus, knowing all that was to befall him, came forward and said to them, 'Whom do you seek?' They answered him, 'Jesus of Nazareth.' Jesus said to them, 'I am he.' (John 18:3–5)

In the darkness of the night, he was not immediately recognised; but such was his presence that when he said 'I am he', they fell back from him. '"I told you that I am he; so, if you seek me, let these men go"' (John 18:8).

Simon – of course it would be Simon – had said he was ready to fight and, if necessary, to die for Jesus. He had come prepared, as John the eye-witness described in vivid detail.

Then Simon Peter, having a sword, drew it and struck the high priest's slave and cut off his right ear. The servant's name was Malchus. Jesus said to Peter, 'Put your sword into its sheath; shall I not drink the cup which the Father has given me?' So the band of soldiers and their captain and the officers of the Jews seized Jesus and bound him. (John 18:10–12)

Drink it he must: the temptation to do otherwise had to be resisted and rejected. The die is cast, and the life of the one who is the Word made Flesh is now in the hands of those who would destroy it.

23

Gethsemane to Golgotha

For all his courage and readiness to die for Jesus – and there can be no doubt that in drawing his sword he was putting his life at risk – Simon Peter was soon to discover his Achilles' heel. Arrested in Gethsemane and bound by the soldiers, Jesus was at first deserted by all his followers. Of them one young man, possibly Mark, since it is he alone who recorded the event, followed the band of soldiers. He had 'nothing but a linen cloth about his body; and they seized him, but he left the linen cloth and ran away naked' (Mark 14:51).

As he ran, embarrassed and confused, he would hear the rough derision of the soldiers ringing in his ears. Yes, it must almost certainly have been Mark himself, for only his continued shame could justify the inclusion of the incident.

Jesus was taken by his captors first to Annas, father-in-law to Caiaphas who was high priest for that year. St John comments that 'It was Caiaphas who had given counsel to the Jews that it was expedient that one man should die for the people' (John 18:14).

Jesus was not entirely alone and deserted by his followers. As the noisy group dragged their captive across the Kidron valley and back to the city, to the court of the high priest, two figures crept quietly behind in the shadows, outside the pool of light formed by the torches of the soldiers. They were Simon Peter and John.

Then in John's account, there is a comment which says more

about its author than it adds to the narrative. Imagine John relating the event to his friends:

'After the soldiers had arrested the Master, Simon Peter and I followed quietly at a distance, out of their sight. When we entered the city I realised they were taking him to the high priest. I'm a good deal younger than old Simon, so I got way ahead of him and caught up with the soldiers. They were too full of what had happened to notice that I'd joined their party.' He went on, with more than a hint of self-importance in his voice, 'Of course I knew the people there and managed to gain entry right into the court itself. I went back and had a word with the maid on duty at the gate and managed to get Simon Peter in as well. But only into the outer court, of course.'

While John was witnessing the interrogation of Jesus by the high priest, Simon Peter remained in the outer court.

And as Peter was below in the courtyard, one of the maids of the high priest came; and seeing Peter warming himself, she looked at him, and said, 'You were also with the Nazarene, Jesus.' But he denied it, saying, 'I neither know nor understand what you mean.' And he went out into the gateway. And the maid saw him, and began to say again to the bystanders, 'This man is one of them.' But again he denied it. And after a little while again the bystanders said to Peter, 'Certainly you are a Galilean.' But he began to invoke a curse on himself and to swear, 'I do not know this man of whom you speak.' And immediately the cock crowed a second time. And Peter remembered how Jesus had said to him, 'Before the cock crows twice, you will deny me three times.' And he broke down and wept. (Mark 14:66–72)

Peter's courage is not in doubt. He was ready to fight against overwhelming odds when Jesus was arrested, knowing that if the soldiers responded he would certainly be killed. He had taken the risk of coming into the city, even into the enemy camp. So what did he fear as he stood warming himself by the fire? The maid may have been present at the arrest; but anyway recognised Peter as one of his followers. When he left the fire to stand by the gateway, she was so certain that she pointed him out to those standing by.

He must have chatted to them, hoping to befriend them and avoid further challenge. But his northern accent gave him away, like a Lancashire lad talking with a group of Cockney taxi-drivers. Tension produces nervous laughter and joking; maybe he joined in their banter, and perhaps he could not face the ridicule he thought would be his lot if he admitted he was a follower of this holy man. 'Who are you then, mate? A Holy Joe come up from the sticks? Enjoy 'ymn-singing, do yer?' Then as the cock crew, the horror of what he had done broke his spirit.

Meanwhile, with John on hand to hear what was happening in the court of the high priest, Jesus was asked about his disciples and his teaching.

> Jesus answered him, 'I have spoken openly to the world; I have always taught in synagogues and in the temple, where all Jews come together; I have said nothing secretly. Why do you ask me? Ask those who have heard me, what I said to them. They know what I said.' (John 18:19–21)

It was a defiant, challenging response; not at all the way one ought to speak to a high priest, and too much for one of the officers standing by, who struck Jesus with his hand – the first of many blows he was to receive – saying, 'Is that how you speak to the high priest?' Jesus turned on him, still defiant.

> 'If I have spoken wrongly, bear witness to the wrong; but if I have spoken rightly, why do you strike me?' Annas then sent him bound to Caiaphas the high priest. (John 18:23–4)

There is some assumption of authority here. Technically, Annas was no longer high priest, having been deposed in about AD 15 by the then procurator, Valerius Gratus, and succeeded by his son-in-law Caiaphas. He seems to have been regarded as still having a share in the high priestly authority, and was perhaps still considered to be high priest by the stricter Jewish leaders. It was to Annas and his courtiers that John was known and he has no record of what happened when Jesus was before Caiaphas. 'Then they led Jesus from the house of Caiaphas to the praetorium. It was early. They themselves did not enter the praetorium, so that they might not be defiled, but might eat the Passover' (John 18:28).

Mark records how, early in the morning, the chief priests, with the elders and scribes, had called a meeting of the council to decide on what should be done with this troublesome prophet. They themselves, as vassals of Rome, lacked authority to put him to death; but Pilate did have that power, if he could be persuaded that Jesus posed a threat to stability in this corner of the Roman empire.

But Pilate was not easily taken in. He mistrusted their motives and their methods, and feared all the time that they would upset the difficult personal balance which he had built up under his procuratorship.

> So Pilate went out to them and said, 'What accusation do you bring against this man?' They answered him, 'If he were not an evil-doer, we would not have handed him over.' Pilate said to them, 'Take him yourselves and judge him by your own law.' The Jews said to him, 'It is not lawful for us to put any man to death.' (John 18:29–31)

The Jewish religious leaders had no real charge to bring against him, at least no charge that would stand up in Roman law; but he was a threat to their position and must be destroyed. Pilate was too shrewd to be taken in by such flimsy evidence. What were they up to? He called Jesus in for a private interrogation. It was a more sympathetic conversation than that with the high priest, and Pilate's first question was the crucial one. 'Are you the king of the Jews?'

> Jesus answered, 'Do you say this of your own accord, or did others say it to you about me?' Pilate answered, 'Am I a Jew? Your own nation and the chief priests have handed you over to me; what have you done?' Jesus answered, 'My kingship is not of this world; if my kingship were of this world, then would my servants fight, that I might not be handed over to the Jews; but my kingship is not from the world.' Pilate said to him, 'So you are a king?' Jesus answered, 'You say that I am a king. For this I was born, and for this I have come into the world, to bear witness to the truth. Every one who is of the truth hears my voice.' (John 18:34-7)

Jesus was telling Pilate, 'My kingdom is no threat to you or to Rome. It is not a kingship of this world at all.' But he is a king? 'You would say that I am a king. You would understand that, and that this was my purpose in coming into the world. What I bear witness to is not power, but truth.' Pilate asks, wryly, 'What is truth?' Perhaps he came to his own career to serve Imperial Rome and the peoples under its care, to establish the *pax Romana*. Time and experience had taught him that the first casualty of the necessary combination of ambition and political pragmatism was truth. But there was enough within him of the desire to exercise a just authority that he refused to condemn a man he saw to be innocent; and a finely honed political cunning and instinct to suspect that the chief priests were setting a trap against his own authority.

> He went out to the Jews again, and told them, 'I find no crime in him. But you have a custom that I should release one man for you at the Passover; will you have me release for you the King of the Jews?' They cried out again, 'Not this man, but Barabbas!' Now Barabbas was a robber.' (John 18:38-40)

St Luke suggests that Barabbas was more than a robber. He

was 'a man who had been thrown into prison for an insurrection started in the city, and for murder' (Luke 23:19). He was, in other words — that is, in our terms and understanding — a terrorist, a person who had killed to further a political end. It was a brilliant stroke on Pilate's part to give them this choice. He would, if they wished, release the one whose kingdom was not of this world, the one who stood for truth, the one who, as Pilate himself recognised, was not a threat to the Roman Empire. Or he would release one who had been convicted for terrorist offences against Rome.

It was for the chief priests and religious leaders of the Jewish nation to choose between the sacred and the secular. Whatever sympathy the chief priests might have had for the political aims of Barabbas — and they did after all expect the Messiah to be a military leader who would rid them of pagan Roman rule — they could not have supported methods, robbery and murder, which were contrary to Mosaic Law. But like many religious leaders since, and not least in our own time, the chief priests were ready to close their eyes to the evils perpetrated by the men of political violence. The judgment of God will be heavy upon them all.

The chief priests persuaded those who had begun to gather on that Passover morning to call not for Jesus but for Barabbas.

> Pilate addressed them once more, desiring to release Jesus; but they shouted out, 'Crucify, crucify him!' A third time he said to them, 'Why, what evil has he done? I have found no crime deserving death; I will therefore chastise him and release him.' But they were urgent, demanding with loud cries that he should be crucified. And their voices prevailed. (Luke 23:22–3)

But Pilate was not content, not yet resigned to submitting to their demands. Maybe if he subjected Jesus to the terrible punishment of the scourge, they would be satisfied. But they were not; nothing would satisfy but the death of Jesus.

> Then Pilate took Jesus and scourged him. And the soldiers plaited a crown of thorns, and put it on his head, and arrayed him in a purple robe; and they came to him, saying, 'Hail, King of the Jews!' and struck him with their hands. Pilate went out again, and said to them, 'Behold, I am bringing him out to you, that you may know that I find no crime in him.' So Jesus came out, wearing the crown of thorns and the purple robe. Pilate said to them, 'Here is the man!' When the chief priests and the officers saw him, they cried out, 'Crucify him, crucify him!' (John 19:1–3)

There have been many attempts by artists to depict this terrible moment. For me, nothing else quite captures the hatred, and the baying of those clamouring for his blood, with the same chilling accuracy of J. S. Bach in his *St John Passion* as the chorus sings out *Kreuzige, kreuzige*, repeated and repeated and repeated.

Still Pilate hesitated to give the final judgment, to utter the death sentence on an innocent man.

> 'Take him yourselves and crucify him, for I find no crime in him.' The Jews answered him, 'We have a law, and by that law he ought to die, because he has made himself the Son of God.' (John 19:6–7)

The charges against Jesus had now taken a new turn, and Pilate was afraid. He knew from his own religion about gods who came down to earth. They were not to be trifled with. Though he may have his own scepticism about it, and though the Jewish gods were not the same as those of Rome, this called for caution.

> When Pilate heard these words, he was the more afraid; he entered the praetorium again and said to Jesus, 'Where are you from?' But Jesus gave no answer. Pilate therefore said to him, 'You will not speak to me? Do you not know that I have power to release you, and power to crucify you?'

Jesus answered him, 'You would have no power over me unless it had been given you from above; therefore he who delivered me to you has the greater sin.' (John 19:8–12)

Here was a prisoner facing a terrible death, yet who remained calm and coolly rational. Instead of grovelling pleas for mercy, instead of excuses and wild promises, bribes and mitigation, there was sympathy and exoneration. Pilate determined that he would not be driven to act against his own instincts; and his instinct was that Jesus was an innocent man. But the chief priests had a final weapon of persuasion.

Upon this Pilate sought to release him, but the Jews cried out, 'If you release this man, you are not Caesar's friend; every one who makes himself a king sets himself against Caesar.' When Pilate heard these words, he brought Jesus out and sat down on the judgement seat at a place called the Pavement, and in Hebrew, Gabbatha. Now it was the day of Preparation of the Passover; it was about the sixth hour. He said to the Jews, 'Here is your King!' They cried out, 'Away with him, away with him, crucify him!' Pilate said to them, 'Shall I crucify your king?' The chief priests answered, 'We have no king but Caesar.' Then he handed him over to them to be crucified. (John 19:12–16)

So judgment was made. Of all things, Pilate could not risk being charged with any kind of betrayal of Caesar. 'If you release this man, you are not Caesar's friend.' There was an implied threat, a coded warning that if Pilate did not do as they asked, then word would reach Caesar of his treachery. 'Everyone who makes himself a king sets himself against Caesar.' It was something Pilate could not risk, and so the King of Kings was condemned to the death of a common criminal, and the Word made Flesh and Judge of all convicted by the words of those who believed they were securing a future for the people of God. Yet in preserving their nation they submitted to a pagan ruler: 'We have no king but Caesar.' It is always the lot of religious leaders who begin to compromise with secular forces and pressures that they are in the end transformed by them.

> So they took Jesus, and he went out, bearing his own cross, to the place called the place of a skull, which is called in Hebrew Golgotha. (John 19:17)

24

The Way of the Cross

When I visited the Holy Land, I carried with me images of Cecil B. de Mille Hollywood biblical epics, and the Good Friday hymn of Mrs Alexander, 'There is a green hill far away without a city wall'. In my mind's eye, the crucifixion took place on one of the brown, dusty hills which surround Jerusalem, and I could visualise the three crosses silhouetted against the sky. Surely the Church of the Holy Sepulchre, right inside the city, in fact well inside the walls of the Old City, could be no more than a convenient place of pilgrimage, a spot hallowed by centuries of devotion by pilgrims eased from the burden of climbing a hill to the actual place of execution.

Yet even with that impression, false as it was, to stand in the chapel of Calvary was an experience which will always be with me. There were few other pilgrims in the city when we were there in mid-1982. Israel had just invaded the Lebanon, and there were sixty no-shows on the flight to Tel Aviv, and we saw many of the sites as few pilgrims ever do, empty of people. So when we visited the Church of the Holy Sepulchre, our small party was able to take in quietly the atmosphere and the associations.

I climbed the steep steps up the block of rock on which is the Calvary chapel, and, for me, to touch its summit through the hole beneath the altar was to be at the place where our salvation was enacted. It was only afterwards that I realised that this was indeed the place of Calvary, that the 'hill' was a rocky outcrop at the gates of the city – ideal for the public display of the fate of miscreants, just as the heads of executed traitors were displayed on poles outside the Tower of London and on old London Bridge. The present Old City does not follow the lines of the city of Jesus' day, and what is now well within those old walls was then outside, but only just outside, by the main road and at one of the main entrances.

> There they crucified him, and with him two others, one on either side, and Jesus between them. Pilate also wrote a title and put it on the cross; it read, 'Jesus of Nazareth, the King of the Jews.' (John 19:18–19)

So Pontius Pilate had the last word. He knew that Jesus was innocent, that he had convicted and sentenced to death a good man, delivered for envy by enemies who had compromised their own faith in order to destroy him. He knew too that he had done so to save his own skin, to avoid the fate which might have befallen him if the leaders of the religious community of the nation had hinted to the Roman secular authorities that their local governor had freed one who claimed the kingdom from Rome. Perhaps he hated himself for this as much as he hated those who had forced him into that position.

> Many of the Jews read this title, for the place where he was crucified was near the city; and it was written in Hebrew, Latin and Greek. The chief priests of the Jews then said to Pilate, 'Do not write, "The King of the Jews", but, "This man said, 'I am the King of the Jews.'"' Pilate answered, 'What I have written, I have written.' (John 19:20–2)

The agony of crucifixion is not merely the searing pain of the nails, tearing into the flesh of wrists and ankles. To breathe, the victim must push himself away from the wood of the cross, so that the nails tear even deeper. For the soldiers it was just another unpleasant job, to be made as light as possible by black humour; and one of the perks was to be able to cast lots for the clothes no longer needed by those executed. They could not have expected Jesus, at the receiving end of the orders they were forced to carry out, to care enough to declare, 'Father, forgive them, for they know not what they do' (Luke 23:34).

Could it be that the officer in charge of them was also the centurion who, witnessing the death of Jesus, was to praise God and say, 'Certainly this man was innocent'? (Luke 23:47) It is probably too fanciful to suggest that he could have been a gentile follower of the Jewish faith, who knew the prophecies of the coming of the Messiah, and who used the colloquial Greek, *dikaios*, meaning 'innocent', in the technical, theological sense of the *Dikaios*, which was a messianic title.

As Jesus hung dying on the cross, he was not free of the taunts of his enemies. Because I have exonerated Pilate at least from some of the blame (though not for his cowardice), I may be charged by the politically correct with anti-Semitism. But 'the Jews' did persuade Pilate, and it was indeed 'the Jews' who could not leave Jesus to die peacefully, but instead mocked him with cries to come down from the cross and so make them believe. There is anti-Semitism neither in this nor in the Scripture from which it is taken. For 'the Jews' is clearly meant in the sense of 'the leaders of the Jews', not the ordinary people but the chief priests, scribes and elders of the Temple.

'The people stood by watching' is St Luke's description, watching perhaps sullenly and helplessly, hating the Romans for what they had done to a good man and hating also their own religious leaders, but not daring, individual by individual, to take any action to express their anger and disgust.

Hearing the religious leaders scoffing at Jesus with cries to come down from the cross that they might believe, one of the criminals vented his own rage against Jesus.

'Are you not the Christ? Save yourself and us!' But the other rebuked him, saying, 'Do you not fear God, since you are under the same condemnation? And we indeed justly; for we are receiving the due reward of our deeds; but this man has done nothing wrong.' And he said, 'Jesus, remember me when you come in your kingly power.' And he said to him, 'Truly, I say to you, today you will be with me in paradise.' (Luke 23:39–43)

For no more than a kind word to a man sharing a cruel, agonising death, the criminal was promised paradise that very day with the Word made Flesh. It is the nature and character of the love which God shows to his children that Jesus offers as a free gift to the criminal. It does not condone whatever sins or crimes have brought him to his fate on Calvary; it does not seek to excuse him or convert him. It is simply love offered and accepted for its own sake. Jesus sees beyond the outward reality to the inner man. We cannot do this because we are not the only Son from the Father; and for us to make a similar statement would not be from love but from sentimentality.

We should be saying to the criminal, 'Oh, come along with us to Paradise. What you have done in the past doesn't matter – God loves you.' Sentimentality ignores the sin, and by ignoring, condones it; God's love on the other hand redeems the sinner. That is the joy of the gospel, and it is the reward of the cross.

As Jesus hung on the cross, he did have friends around him, and William Temple identified them as 'Mary the mother of the Lord and her sister, Salome, the mother of the Beloved Disciple; also Mary the wife of Cleopas (brother, according to Hegisippus, of St Joseph) and Mary Magdalene; and among them was the Beloved Disciple, the son of Salome, the nephew of the Blessed Virgin and cousin of the Lord.' (*Readings in St John's Gospel*, p. 367)

It was a personal, family moment, a time to set matters aright for the future.

When Jesus saw his mother, and the disciple whom he loved standing near, he said to his mother, 'Woman, behold, your son!' Then he said to the disciple, 'Behold, your mother!' And from that hour the disciple took her to his own home. (John 19:26–7)

It was nearly the end. A dry whisper came from the mouth of Jesus: 'I thirst.' It was the one acknowledgment of human need, from the one who was both human and divine.

> A bowl of vinegar stood there; so they put a sponge full of the vinegar on hyssop and held it to his mouth. When Jesus had received the vinegar, he said, 'It is finished'; and he bowed his head and gave up his spirit. (John 19:29–30)

Consummatum est! It is finished. From the moment when the creature made in the image of the Creator first chose evil rather than good (and there must have been a moment in the millennia of time when that choice was first made by the creature with free will, with the freedom to choose), God had set in course His purpose that the broken relationship should be restored. The sacrifice on the cross was the fulfilment of that plan and purpose, and now it was indeed finished, completed, consummated.

But for the broken body of Jesus, there was a final possible indignity. Because a crucified person, in order to breathe, needed to be able to push himself away from the cross to let the air into his lungs, it was customary to make sure of death by breaking the victim's legs. Again it was the religious leaders who sought Pilate's authority that this might be done.

> Since it was the day of Preparation, in order to prevent the bodies from remaining on the cross on the sabbath (for that sabbath was a high day), the Jews asked Pilate that their legs might be broken, and that they might be taken away. So the soldiers came and broke the legs of the first, and of the other who had been crucified with him; but when they came to Jesus and saw that he was already dead, they did not break his legs. But one of the soldiers pierced his side with a spear, and at once there came out blood and water. (John 19:32–4)

Now he must be taken down from the cross and buried. It has always been the lot of those who have been prepared to put their heads above the parapet and challenge the establishment, Jewish, Christian, or whatever, that others will come secretly with the assurance, 'Of course, I'm with you on this. You can be sure of my support. But of course I'll have to keep very quiet about it.' This is a kind of cowardice, a discretion which is never the better part of valour. Nicodemus was one such and so was Joseph of Arimathea. St John told of Nicodemus, earlier in the story of Jesus and his ministry.

> Now there was a man of the Pharisees, named Nicodemus, a ruler of the Jews. This man came to Jesus by night and said to him, 'Rabbi, we know that you are a teacher come from God; for no one can do these signs that you do, unless God is with him.' Jesus answered him, 'Truly, truly, I say to you, unless one is born anew, he cannot see the kingdom of God.' (John 3:1–3)

But Nicodemus rejected the new birth which was required of him and makes no further appearance until after the crucifixion. Joseph too was a disciple of Jesus, 'but secretly, for fear of the Jews' (John 19:38); and according to St Luke, 'He was a member of the council, a good and righteous man, who had not consented to their purpose and deed, and he was looking for the kingdom of God' (Luke 23:50–1).

Perhaps they now felt a responsibility, guilty at their silence and the secrecy of their support for Jesus. Whatever the reason, Joseph plucked up sufficient courage to go to Pilate for permission to take away the body of Jesus. Nicodemus too, oblivious now to the possibility of criticism from his fellow Pharisees, 'came bringing a mixture of myrrh and aloes, about a hundred pounds weight. They took the body of Jesus, and bound it in linen cloths with the spices, as is the burial custom of the Jews' (John 19:39–40).

Before taking charge of the operation, one must assume that out of courtesy they would have sought the permission of Mary, his mother, and of those who had followed Jesus to the cross.

Now in the place where he was crucified there was a garden, and in the garden a new tomb where no one had ever been laid. So, because of the Jewish day of Preparation, as the tomb was close at hand, they laid Jesus there. (John 23:41–2)

Mary of Magdala watched in her grief, comforted by Mary the wife of Cleopas, as the body was laid in the tomb, and as a great stone was rolled to close the entrance to the tomb. The chief priests remained unsatisfied and nervous. Remembering that Jesus had said, 'After three days I will rise again', they petitioned Pilate that he would put a guard on the tomb until after the third day

'lest his disciples go and steal him away, and tell the people, "He has risen from the dead," and the last fraud will be worse than the first.' Pilate said to them, 'You have a guard of soldiers; go, make it as secure as you can.' So they went and made the sepulchre secure by sealing the stone and setting a guard. (Matthew 27:64–6)

All that could be done had been done. It was too late to complete the full burial requirement before the onset of the sabbath day, and the disciples went their way submerged in a hopeless grief. It was all over, finished. If Jesus had really been the Messiah, his enemies had killed him; and if he were not – well, anyway he was dead. Like every bereavement, life would never be the same again; and the life they had lived with him, and yes, had enjoyed – for the excitement of ministry, and the joy of his presence – had now come to an end. Soon they would have to pick up the pieces and return to what they had been – fishermen, tax-collectors, housewives.

On the sabbath they rested according to the commandment. (Luke 32:56)

25

Hell and Damnation

I am there at Calvary, at the crucifixion.

I am there in the soldiers, not knowing what they are doing
to the Prince of Peace, forgiven even when they do not know
the nature of their sin.

I am there in the hangers-on, seeking admiration from those
whose favour they covet as they mock him in his suffering.

I am there in the chief priests and elders, in the leaders of the
religious establishment, who for expediency and for the
preservation of their own position, put the secular before
the sacred.

I am there in the crowds, those ordinary people of the faith who
can only look on helplessly as their leaders destroy the one
who is the Truth, fearful to step out of line, comfortable in heir
own little world yet horrified at what is done in   their name.

I am there in those whose interest is only academic, curious to
see what a dying man will do, how he will react to this or to that.

I am there in the centurion, believing because he knows what
he has seen.

I am there in Joseph and Nicodemus, covering their shame at
inaction with a final tribute.

I am there in Mary the mother, in Mary the neighbour and in
Mary the sinner restored.

I am there in them all, for it was for my sins and for theirs
that he died.

*   *   *

But I cannot be there in the bereavement and emptiness of Holy Saturday, that sabbath day after the crucifixion, because I know the end of the story.

'On the sabbath day they rested according to the command-ment,' St Luke (Luke 23:56) tells us. Perhaps they gathered in the upper room where some had met for the final meal. There would be much anguish, much weeping, and not only from his mother Mary and from Mary of Magdala. Peter would be inconsolable at his denials, and the other disciples little less so since they had all forsaken him and fled.

Those who were not at the cross were maybe in hiding, coming intermittently and surreptitiously to where they imag-ined their friends would be gathering, careful to keep the sabbath law. There would be anger too, and bitter recrimi-nations, exploding in the tension of the day and subsiding in yet deeper remorse.

But what of Jesus. In the creed we say that after the crucifixion, he 'descended into hell'. He had told the criminal on the cross, 'Today you will be with me in Paradise' (Luke 23:43); and Peter in his first letter writes:

For Christ also died for sins once for all, the righteous for the unrighteous, that he might bring us to God, being put to death in the flesh but alive in the spirit; in which he went and preached to the spirits in prison, who formerly did not obey, when God's patience waited in the days of Noah. (1 Peter 3:18–20)

Eternity touches time at every point, and the death of Christ on the cross was for all, living and departed, not just for those alive then or those to come but for all who sought to come to God. The descent into 'hell' is generally taken to refer to a visit by Christ to the realm of existence, neither heaven nor hell in the final sense, but a state of being where those 'waited' who had lived before the coming of the Christian gospel.

It is fashionable to dismiss the concept of hell altogether, at least of a hell that is of fire and brimstone, of eternal torment for lost souls. But we are creatures given a choice by our Creator, a choice between whether to serve Him or whether to reject Him, a choice between good and evil. If there is any reality to that free will then it must in theory be possible to make a choice against God, to prefer utter evil to total good.

If we love the children we have brought into the world, we love them as they are, that is in however tiny a measure, as God loves us who are His children. We bring them up to know right and wrong and do not cease to love them if they choose to do wrong. Yet we do not have ultimate control over them, and they could choose to have nothing more to do with us. And the totality of that breakage of relationship between parent and child might be such that the child would feel it impossible to return, even if he or she wished, and though the parent might hope for nothing less.

It would be painful and we would not cease to love them; but they have the right and the power and the free will to make that choice. If there is not a possibility of eternal separation from God, then we do not have free will. The suffering of Christ on the cross contained the ultimate pain of that separation; as it must if he were to experience the fullness of human agony.

> And when the sixth hour had come, there was darkness over the land until the ninth hour. And at the ninth hour, Jesus cried with a loud voice, '*Eloi, Eloi, lama sabachthani?*' which means, 'My God, my God, why hast thou forsaken me?' (Mark 15:33–4)

As he hung in agony on the cross, he comforted himself with the words of the Psalmist, and the psalm which begins with those words is a psalm about the abiding presence of God.

> Whither shall I go then from they Spirit:
>> or whither shall I go then from they presence?
> If I climb up into heaven, thou art there:
>> if I go down to hell, thou art there also.
> If I take the wings of the morning:

and remain in the uttermost parts of the earth;
Even there also shall they hand lead me:
   and thy right hand shall hold me.
If I say, Peradventure the darkness shall cover me:
   then shall my night be turned to day.
Yea, the darkness is no darkness with thee, but the night is
   as clear as the day:
   the darkness and light to thee are both alike.

           (Psalm 139: 6–11, Book of Common Prayer)

As Jesus uttered the opening words of the psalm, 'My God, my God, why hast thou forsaken me?', he felt not the abiding presence of the Father, but the utter desolation and emptiness of His absence. The Ancient of Days who had come down to earth experienced the totality of separation from the ground of His own being. That is not a feeling of non-being. It was suggested recently that hell is in reality non-being, but this is to sentimentalise a painful religious truth.

We need to picture that which we have not seen or experienced in terms of that which we know. A science fiction writer will describe an alien, which he has not seen, in terms of a life-form which he knows – a giant slug, a life-size horned ant; or the alien will never be seen at all in the narrative. Writers and theologians and painters have treated hell in the same way. The Jewish hell, Gehenna, was hot and fiery, like the ever-burning, evil-smelling rubbish pits of the Hinnom valley outside Jerusalem. The Greek hell was icy, the worst they could contemplate.

But no description could do full justice to the pain of eternal separation from the God of Love, with the knowledge that the separation was not His will but one's own personal choice.

Occasionally and only for a brief moment before experience reminds me of all that God has done for me, and how I have known the reality of His love and His presence, just for that moment I wonder if it is all a mistake, that after death I shall end in nothingness. In my heart I know that this cannot be; but if it were so, it holds no fear for me, for I would know nothing of it. I would on death become a non-being; I would be a live sentient being – and then nothing, not even blackness. That condition of non-being is not hell.

Hell is to cry, 'My God, my God, why hast thou forsaken me?' and to know that He has not forsaken me but that I have forsaken Him. Only God Himself knows if any of even the most evil of His children has made that choice, in the full and total knowledge of what God is and does.

But hell is a reality, even if it is empty.

26

Resurrection and Life

To Martha at the death of Lazarus, Jesus said,

'I am the resurrection and the life; he who believes in me,
though he die, yet shall he live, and whoever lives and
believes in me shall never die. Do you believe this?' She
said to him, 'Yes, Lord; I believe that you are the Christ,
the Son of God, he who is coming into the world.' (John
11:25–7)

St Paul wrote to the church at Corinth,

If Christ has not been raised, your faith is futile and you are
still in your sins. Then those also who have fallen asleep in
Christ have perished. If in this life only we have hope in
Christ, we are of all men most to be pitied. (1 Corinthians
15:17–19)

To those to whom he preached and who asked him for a sign,
Jesus said,

'This generation is an evil generation; it seeks a sign, but
no sign shall be given to it except the sign of Jonah. For
as Jonah became a sign to the men of Nineveh, so will the
Son of man be to this generation.' (Luke 11:29–30)

The resurrection is the sign, the one proof for those who will see, that Jesus is all that he claimed to be. If it is not true, or if after the third day, Jesus was 'alive' simply in the minds of his followers, then everything of the faith collapses.

Joseph of Arimathea and Nicodemus had not completed the burial necessities by the time that the sabbath began on the evening of the sixth day of the week. At the earliest opportunity on the day we call Sunday – 'while it was still dark', John tells us (John 20:1) – the women slipped out of the city early, across the road by one of the main gates and opposite the mound of Calvary where the crucifixion had taken place, to the garden where in a new tomb the body of Jesus had been laid, with a stone rolled across to seal it and a guard posted. John mentions only Mary Magdalene; Luke includes with her Joanna and Mary, the mother of James.

Finding that the stone had been removed and fearing the body had been stolen, Mary ran back to where Simon Peter and John were staying.

> 'They have taken the Lord out of the tomb, and we do not know where they have laid him.' Peter then came out with the other disciple, and they went toward the tomb. They both ran, but the other disciple outran Peter and reached the tomb first; and stooping to look in, he saw the linen cloths lying there, but he did not go in. (John 20:2–5)

The younger and fitter John outrunning Peter but not going into the tomb; then Peter stumbling there, out of breath, and pushing past John to go right into the tomb, both of them dumb-struck by this new development, their hearts pounding at the effort and with the horror they felt, wondering if the religious authorities had now even stooped to defiling their master's last resting place.

Inside the tomb, Simon Peter saw no signs of entry or hasty removal. The linen cloths in which the body had been wrapped were lying in their place, and the napkin which had been about his head neatly rolled up and not lying with the linen cloths. That puzzled him. It did not bear the marks of a grave robbery.

John in his account, being John, says that 'he saw and believed'. 'Of course as soon as I saw the linen cloths and the napkin, I knew straight away what had happened – that he had risen from the dead'; though, as he says in his gospel, at this time they did not understand the Scripture that he must rise from the dead. Then the two of them went back to where they were staying.

Mary remained behind, perhaps alone, perhaps still with the other women, refusing to leave. When a little later she rushed to where the disciples were, she had a tale to tell – something like this.

You won't believe what has happened. After you'd gone, I stooped down to look into the tomb, and – I tell no lie – there they were, two angels in white, asking why I was crying. 'Because they've taken away my Lord, and I don't know where they've laid him.' Then I turned round and saw a man standing there – I thought it was the gardener. He asked me why I was crying and who I was looking for. Well, I didn't know who he was, and it was still not quite light, and I was all confused and upset, so I said, 'If you've carried him away, just tell me where he is and I'll take him away and bury him again.' Then I looked again, and he looked at me, and he said, 'Mary.' Just quietly, just like that. 'Teacher!' I said, and tried to hold him, but he told me to come back and tell you something about him ascending and going to the Father.

They would hardly believe her; would perhaps humour and comfort her. 'Yes, of course you did, Mary. Now, come along and sit down, and have a hot drink; and you'll feel a lot better.' 'Poor Mary, she's so upset, we must keep an eye on her for the next few days.'

Later that day, two of the disciples were walking back to their village, Emmaus, some seven miles to the west of

Jerusalem. One was Cleopas and the other, though unnamed, was almost certainly his wife, Mary, who had stood with Mary the mother of Jesus at the cross. Deep in conversation, they were joined by a stranger whom they did not recognise. There was nothing miraculous in this failure.

Meet someone well known but out of context and it is a familiar experience not to be certain of recognition. You see a face on a bus or a train, or away on holiday, familiar and yet not familiar. Perhaps it is someone who works in a shop, or a not-too-close neighbour, someone who occasionally sits on a committee. But they are not where they should be, where you would know them without even thinking about it, and you look at them. 'I'm sure I know that face; but no, it can't be, I'm mistaken, and anyway I can't even put a name to them.'

The two on the road to Emmaus did not expect to see Jesus and so they failed to recognise him, being anyway deep in their own thoughts and discussions. They were less than pleased at the stranger's question, What were they discussing?

And they stood still, looking sad. Then one of them, named Cleopas, answered him, 'Are you the only visitor to Jerusalem who does not know the things that have happened there in these days?' (Luke 24:18)

What things were these? So they told him, told him of the great prophet Jesus of Nazareth, of how the chief priests and rulers delivered him up to death, and crucified him, of how they had hoped he was the one sent to redeem Israel. Then they looked at each other. Ought they to tell the stranger the latest news, the strange story brought by Mary of Magdala? They took a breath and decided to risk his incredulity and maybe ridicule at what they had to tell, of the women going to the tomb and saying they saw Jesus, alive.

And he said to them, 'O foolish men, and slow of heart to believe all that the prophets have spoken! Was it not necessary that the Christ should suffer these things and enter into his glory?' And beginning with Moses and all the prophets, he interpreted to them in all the scriptures the things concerning himself. (Luke 24:25–7)

By this time, they were on the outskirts of Emmaus, at the end of their journey. It was late in the day, towards evening, and they invited him to stay at their home.

So he went with them into the house. When he was at table with them, he took bread and blessed, and broke it, and gave it to them. And their eyes were opened and they recognised him; and he vanished out of their sight. (Luke 24:29–31)

We all have our personal characteristics, mannerisms, or some turn of phrase which immediately identifies us; features which are grist to the mill of impressionists. So particular to Jesus was the use of the phrase translated for us as 'Truly, truly, I say to you' that the Greek text of the New Testament retained the Aramaic 'Amen, Amen' which he actually spoke. Moreover, always it precedes a statement of importance.

It was this that was familiar in what he said. In what he did, it was the manner of his taking, blessing, breaking and giving – at the feeding of the five thousand and of the four thousand; at the Last Supper; now at the evening meal at the house in Emmaus. And of course for us, when we take and bless and break and give, or are given, the holy Bread of the Eucharist.

They said to each other, 'Did not our hearts burn within us while he talked to us on the road, while he opened the scriptures?' And they rose that same hour and returned to Jerusalem; and they found the eleven gathered together, and those who were with them, who said, 'The Lord has risen indeed, and has appeared to Simon!' Then they told what had happened on the road, and how he was known to them in the breaking of the bread. (Luke 24:32–5)

They were excited, happy yet puzzled at the news, some no doubt wondering if it were really true, if there was not alongside the collective grief some kind of collective hallucination as well. The disciples at Emmaus had sat with Jesus for an early evening meal, and then walked back to Jerusalem, a journey on foot of perhaps one and a half to two hours. The next appearance was later still on that same evening.

> On the evening of that day, the first day of the week, the doors being shut where the disciples were, for fear of the Jews, Jesus came and stood among them and said to them, 'Peace be with you.' And when he had said this, he showed them his hands and his side. Then the disciples were glad when they saw the Lord. Jesus said to them again, 'Peace be with you. As the Father has sent me, even so I send you.' And when he had said this, he breathed on them and said to them, 'Receive the Holy Spirit. If you forgive the sins of any, they are forgiven; if you retain the sins of any, they are retained.' (John 20:19–23)

Thomas, nicknamed 'the Twin', was absent on that first day. They told him that Jesus was alive; but he was a rational, sensible man, not easily persuaded by the unexpected and irrational. And it was irrational that someone whom they had seen die could rise from the dead. What would convince him?

> 'Unless I see in his hands the print of the nails, and place my finger in the mark of the nails, and place my hand in his side, I will not believe.' (John 20:25)

A week later, Thomas was with them in the house when Jesus came again and stood among them.

> 'Peace be with you.' Then he said to Thomas, 'Put your finger here, and see my hands; and put out your hand, and place it in my side; do not be faithless, but believing.'

Thomas answered him, 'My Lord and my God!' (John 20:26–8)

A few years ago in Holy Week, BBC Television presented a dramatic reading of the Passion stories in the Gospels, with six actors reading and acting out the events. Switching of characters between the actors made it less successful than it might have been, but for me one moment stood out – this encounter between Jesus and doubting Thomas. Timothy West played Thomas, and as Jesus invited him to touch and to feel, a look passed between them and Thomas fell at his feet, held his hands, and in a voice which held both awe and penitence, he whispered, 'My Lord and my God!'

It is a moment for every Christian, when reasonable doubt is transformed into the combination of belief and trust which is faith, when we see and understand and know that it is all real and vital and life-enhancing. But we cannot see and touch, we can only know what he has done for us, and trust the accounts others have who were with him – as Thomas could not.

Jesus said to him, 'Have you believed because you have seen me? Blessed are those who have not seen and yet believe.' (John 20:29)

On the northerly shore of the Sea of Galilee, not far from Capernaum, at Tabgha is the Church of the Primacy of Peter, and by it, an open-air chapel with, if I remember aright, a central altar. Certainly we celebrated the Eucharist there, at a site venerated as the place of the appearance of the risen Christ by the lakeside.

Overjoyed as the disciples were at his rising from the dead, they knew they had let him down badly. How could he trust them again? Whatever plans he might have to continue his ministry and teaching they surely could have no part in it. Life for them would have to return to what it had been.

Simon Peter, Thomas called the Twin, Nathanael of Cana

in Galilee, the sons of Zebedee, and two others of his disciples were together. Simon Peter said to them, 'I am going fishing.' They said to him, 'We will go with you.' They went out and got into the boat; but that night they caught nothing. Just as day was breaking, Jesus stood on the beach; yet the disciples did not know that it was Jesus. Jesus said to them, 'Children, have you any fish?' They answered him, 'No.' He said to them, 'Cast the net on the right side of the boat, and you will find some.' So they cast it, and now they were not able to haul it in, for the quantity of the fish. (John 21:4–6)

It was not the first time there had been a miraculous catch of fishes. Before Jesus had called Simon Peter to be one of his disciples, he had borrowed Simon's boat to preach to the crowds on the shore of the lake. Afterwards he told Simon to sail to the deeper water and let down his nets. Simon, on being told how to do his own job by an outsider, grumbled a little but gave in, maybe reluctantly.

'Master, we toiled all night and caught nothing! But at your word I will let down the nets.' And when they had done this, they enclosed a great shoal of fish. (Luke 5:5)

So great was the catch that they had to call their partners to help, and even then both boats began to sink at the weight of the catch. 'Have nothing to do with me, Lord,' cried Peter. 'I am a sinful man.'

'Do not be afraid; henceforth you will be catching men.' And when they had brought their boats to land, they left everything and followed him. (Luke 5:10–11)

John, one of the sons of Zebedee, had been present at this earlier event and remembered. 'It's the Lord!' he told Simon Peter; and Simon Peter jumped into the sea and swam to the shore, as the others struggled to bring in the catch.

When they got out on land, they saw a charcoal fire there, with fish lying on it, and bread. Jesus said to them, 'Bring some of the fish you have just caught.' So Simon Peter went aboard and hauled the net ashore, full of large fish, a hundred and fifty-three of them; and although there were so many, the net was not torn. Jesus said to them, 'Come and have breakfast.' Now none of the disciples dared ask him, 'Who are you?' They knew it was the Lord. Jesus came and took the bread and gave it to them, and so with the fish. (John 21:9–13)

The first miraculous catch was followed by the call to leave their nets and become 'fishers of men'. But that was before he knew their weakness, so surely it could not happen again. Simon Peter carried the greatest guilt for his denials, and it was to him that Jesus must give assurance. After breakfast, Jesus asked him, gently, 'Simon, son of John, do you love me more than these?'

Our language does not have the same nuances as those recorded in the Greek text of this event, and when Simon (not for the moment here in the narrative called 'Simon Peter' – the Rock) answers Jesus, 'Yes, Lord, you know that I love you,' he uses a verb for 'love' (*phileo*) which is less strong in its meaning than the *agapao* which Jesus himself used. Again Jesus asked him, 'Simon, son of John, do you *agapais* me?' Again Simon responded with the lesser word for love: 'You know I care about you, that I'm your friend.'

Love, as St Paul was to write later to the church at Corinth, 'bears all things, believes all things, hopes all things, endures all things' (1 Corinthians 13:7). That was not how Simon dared describe his own affection for Jesus, because he had denied he even knew him at the moment of his greatest need. And what is more, Jesus had known he would do just that. So again he responded with the word of lesser meaning.

But then Jesus asked the question a third time, now using that weaker verb. Peter was grieved that this time he asked him, 'Do you *phileo* me?' 'Lord,' he said, with a sad and hurt indignation, 'you know all things. You surely do know that I care about you, that I am your friend, even if I cannot now say I would endure all for you.' After each response from Simon, Jesus said to him, 'Feed my sheep.'

Peter is restored. In spite of all that he, and all who had been called and chosen, had done (save the traitor Judas, now dead by his own hand), there was still a task for them – in fact, the very same task to which he had first called them. But there would be a harsh price to pay, for his call is always a call to bear a cross, and in Peter's case this would be literally true.

> Jesus said to him, 'Feed my sheep. Truly, truly, I say to you, when you were young, you girded yourself and walked where you would; but when you are old, you will stretch out your hands, and another will gird you and carry you where you do not wish to go.' (John 21:17–18)

Even now, the old Peter is only a little below the surface. As soon as he had been restored by Jesus, he noticed John following close behind them.

> 'Lord, what about this man?' Jesus said to him, 'If it is my will that he remain until I come, what is that to you? Follow me!' (John 21:21–2)

The call and purpose of God for another is not our concern; we have our own call to fulfil and that is enough. Simon Peter's call was to end, in this life, in Rome, carried by others to where he would not go, just as Jesus promised, crucified like his Master, though head downwards at his own request, unworthy to die in the same manner as his Lord.

Though not often to a physical crucifixion, our call is the same as that given to those first disciples, in the words of Jesus to them at Caesarea Philippi:

> 'If any man would come after me, let him take up his cross and follow me. For whoever would save his life will lose

it, and whoever loses his life for my sake will find it. For what will it profit a man, if he gains the whole world and forfeits his life? Or what shall a man give in return for his life?' (Matthew 16:24–6)

We can waste the opportunity, we can misuse the purpose, we can reject the strength God offers in its fulfilment; but the call we cannot avoid, whatever we may do with it, and whoever we are. We should request only one epitaph when our task is completed; not that we can be called successful, only that we have been faithful.

27

The End and the Beginning

Jesus rose from the dead bodily. He met and talked with his disciples, walked the road to Emmaus with two of them, ate broiled fish with them on the day of his resurrection, was touched by Thomas, made breakfast for them by the lakeside. He was no ghost, nor merely a vivid memory in their tortured, bereaved minds. An hallucination would not have satisfied Thomas, nor restored Peter. He seems to have come and gone as he pleased, and been recognised or unrecognised according to circumstance.

But real, living, bodily, he most certainly was, even though in what St Paul calls a 'glorified' body. 'What is sown is perishable, what is raised is imperishable. It is sown in dishonour, it is raised in glory. It is sown in weakness, it is raised in power. It is sown a physical body, it is raised a spiritual body' (1 Corinthians 15:42–4).

We make a mistake of language if we understand 'spiritual' as 'less than natural'. Rather its meaning is 'supernatural' – something which is greater than that which we know of the natural and physical.

In being raised from the dead, Christ has shown us the way we shall eventually follow.

But in fact Christ has been raised from the dead, the first fruits of those who have fallen asleep. For as by a man came death, by a man has come also the resurrection of the dead. For as in Adam all die, so in Christ shall all be made alive. But each in his own order: Christ the first fruits, then at his coming those who belong to Christ. Then comes the end, when he delivers the kingdom to God the Father after destroying every rule and every authority and every power. For he must reign until he has put all his enemies under his feet. The last enemy to be destroyed is death. (1 Corinthians 15:20–6)

Such majestic words, used so many times at funeral services to bring comfort to the bereaved, give the hope for eternity. Those who have died have not, in the words of Shakespeare, reached an 'undiscover'd country from whose bourn no traveller returns', but have simply travelled beyond that horizon which is the limit of our earthly sight. Death is not to be feared as a cruel enemy, but welcomed as a friend. For as Christ died and rose so shall we rise, to be reunited for all eternity with those whom we have loved in this life and from whom by death we have for a time been separated.

How this can be, I cannot tell; but I know it to be true, as surely as I know that day succeeds night. I know it because I trust the One who said this would be so. In the meantime, we live according to his purpose in this life, remembering that it is a preparation for life eternal, remembering that we have a task to perform, remembering that he has called us, strengthened us, guided us, fed us, throughout this journey on which he has placed us.

There is much that we cannot know and much that we should not ask. Let St Paul have the final word:

When I came to you, brethren, I did not come proclaiming to you the testimony of God in lofty words or wisdom. For I decided to know nothing among you except Jesus Christ and him crucified. And I was with you in weakness and much trembling; and my speech and my message were not in plausible words of wisdom, but in demonstration of the Spirit and power, that your faith might not rest in the wisdom of men but in the power of God. Yet among the mature we do impart wisdom, although it is not a wisdom of this age or of the rulers of this age, who are doomed to pass away. But we impart a hidden wisdom of God, which God decreed before the ages for our glorification. None of the rulers of this age understood this; for if they had, they would not have crucified the Lord of glory. But as it is written, *'What no eye has seen, nor ear heard, nor the heart of man conceived, what God has prepared for those who love him,'* God has revealed to us through the Spirit. *For the Spirit searches everything, even the depths of God.* (1 Corinthians 2:1–10)